CONTENTS

◆ CHAPTER SIX

◆ CHAPTER SEVEN

THE MAGICIAN

THE HANGED MAN

INTRODUCTION

I f you want insight into your love life, career potential, or what your future holds—or if you just want to understand yourself better—look no further than tarot cards. For centuries, people around the world have consulted tarot in order to discover the secrets of the universe. With *The Only Tarot Book You'll Ever Need*, you can do the same.

One of the wonderful things about tarot is that the cards present images that trigger memories, passions, and dreams you already hold inside you. Plus, anyone can use them—you don't need any special training beyond what you'll read in this book. Tarot's purpose is to help you probe your own subconscious and to find answers within yourself. The cards speak to the creative part of your mind, the part that serves as the architect of your life, to guide you in making choices.

Tarot cards can help you answer questions big and small. Is your relationship built to last? Is your current job a dead end or a stepping-stone to greater things? Should you try to reconcile with that old friend or let the friendship go? The scenarios, colors, and numbers shown on the cards will expand your vision and allow you to figure out which paths to take…while learning more about yourself in the process. It's easy to fit tarot into your busy life—whether you simply draw a single tarot card as a daily morning ritual for receiving guidance, or deal spreads when you have specific questions to ask.

This book provides all the fundamentals you need to start reading tarot. First, you'll find a tarot deck that's right for you and discover different ways to incorporate tarot into your life. Next, you'll learn what all the images and numbers on the cards mean. Then you'll find explanations of the standard interpretations of each card, which will give you a framework that enables you to develop your own, personal dialogue with the cards. Finally, you'll practice how to use "spreads"—groupings of cards that tell a story. Spreads let you see the links between past, present, and future—how your thoughts and actions manifest your reality.

Best of all, tarot encourages you to open your mind and your heart. Explore. Engage your curiosity. Use your imagination. And, most importantly, enjoy yourself. Tarot isn't just for answering serious questions; it can help with smaller, everyday issues as well. Let tarot shine light into your inner self and help you live your best life, now. ◆

Chapter

1

INTRODUCTION TO TAROT

A BRIEF HISTORY OF TAROT

The mystery of tarot's origins is part of its allure. The earliest-known cards date from the fifteenth century and are known collectively as the Visconti-Sforza Tarot. Incomplete versions of these decks are located in libraries and museums across the world. The first entire deck still in existence was painted by the Italian artist Bonifacio Bembo for the Duke of Milan.

There are many theories about how tarot got its start, and each one is compelling. One theory is set in the great library of Alexandria in Egypt, where a female librarian named Hypatia was world-renowned for her wisdom and knowledge. In this library, they kept scrolls that were said to contain all the knowledge of the ancient world. Among these scrolls was the legendary Book of Thoth, derived from the schools of ancient Egypt. Some say that the allegorical illustrations on tarot cards contain the secret teachings found in the Book of Thoth, with the Major Arcana representing a course in personal and spiritual development. If that is the case, tarot cards distill information from an ancient Egyptian textbook.

The Minor Arcana, which was added to tarot at a later date, may have derived from an Italian card game known as tarocchi. Our present-day poker decks closely resemble the Minor Arcana of the tarot. Some cartomancers (people who use cards for divination) use standard playing cards for their readings.

Tarot images in general are deeply linked to ancient beliefs, mythologies, and religious systems such as the Hebrew kabbalah. The cards' numerological associations have been tied to the Greek mathematician Pythagoras, who taught that letters and numbers contain divine essence and extraordinary powers unrealized by the uninitiated.

Romani people may have carried the cards to Europe. (The term *Gypsy* is considered to be a corrupt form of the word *Egyptian*.) The Catholic Church, however, believed tarot was "the devil's picture book" and quickly condemned the cards as heretical. To possess them was dangerous. Thus during the Middle Ages, tarot went underground, along with astrology and many other forms of occult knowledge. (*Occult* simply means "hidden.")

The knowledge contained in tarot continued to be passed down in secret, until interest in the cards surfaced again during the Renaissance.

Though its true history may never be known, it's clear that tarot cards have been advising and guiding people for ages. The amazing insights contained in tarot and the deck's inherent flexibility make it just as relevant during contemporary times as it was centuries ago.

WHAT'S IN A TAROT DECK?

A typical tarot deck consists of seventy-eight cards. Of these, the first twenty-two are called the Major Arcana. (*Arcana* is a fancy word for "mysteries" or "secrets.") The fifty-six remaining cards are called the Minor Arcana, presumably because they contain information that is of a less important or less mystical nature. Because tarot can be understood as a complete body of wisdom and guidance, it is sometimes thought of as a book—or, more accurately, as two books—of knowledge.

The Major Arcana

The Major Arcana are the hallmark of any tarot deck. These cards are said to represent the mysteries or secrets of the universe. As such, they are the most complex cards in the entire tarot deck and require the most time and effort to fully understand. Each of the Major Arcana cards, which are also often called trumps, contains a picture that includes many different symbols or scenarios. The pictures depicted on tarot cards can differ stylistically from deck to deck, but the main symbols are basically the same in all decks. Each of the Major Arcana cards has a title, such as The Magician, The Empress, The Lovers,

The Moon, The Tower, and so on. They are numbered from zero (The Fool) to twenty-one (The World).

There is a disagreement among various schools of thought regarding what the Major Arcana was originally developed for and how it was used. Some scholars and authors focus primarily on the numerical order of the cards (zero to twenty-one), believing that they show the development of an individual's life. Some interpreters have placed psychological meanings onto the Major Arcana, while others have viewed them as representing spiritual development and growth.

The Major Arcana cards also describe a path to enlightenment—The Fool's Journey. The Fool's Journey is a story that begins with The Fool representing innocence and the initial step of the journey, and ends with The World, which signifies wisdom and completion. This journey through the twenty-two cards of the Major Arcana can be used as an allegorical story of personal spiritual awakening. Learning this story through tarot can help you understand your own spiritual journey and learn your current position in it. This knowledge can inspire you to tap into your true potential and realize the possibilities that await you.

The Connection to a Higher Being

The cards in the Major Arcana can be looked at as the "big picture" cards. They show overarching themes in your life and represent forces that may seem beyond your control. Depending on your personal worldview, you could think of these forces as fate, god, goddess, universe, spirit guides, karma, or your own higher self. Whichever way you choose to see the energies or entities behind the cards, they indicate that something larger, outside yourself, is influencing you and the issue about which you are seeking advice.

When many trumps turn up in a reading, it's a signal that the situation is not entirely in your own hands or that you are not alone in the matter that concerns you. Higher forces outside your control may be at work, perhaps guiding the outcome. Basically, fate has the upper hand in the situation. In some cases, a predominance of trump cards shows that previous actions or decisions have already set things in motion, and now the situation is out of your control—you must wait for external forces to play out and decide the outcome.

The Major Arcana cards contain many different layers and possibilities to their definitions. As you work with them, these layers reveal themselves. For example, on a strictly practical level, The Empress may be a direct reference to your mother or your desire to become a mother. On the mundane level, The Magician may refer to your desire to live a more creative life, to be more creative in your work. On the level of spiritual development, The Devil may indicate that it is time for you to throw off the obstacles that are preventing your living more fully and deeply, that you should tend to your soul needs rather than your material concerns.

Your life will unfold according to your own inner blueprint and pace. There's no hurrying the process, which ultimately takes place on its own time schedule, no matter how much you try to push it and make it happen faster. Paying attention to the cycles in your life will show you the patterns that you are following and may suggest new and different directions. The Major Arcana can be a guide that helps you to explore these universal concepts and patterns as they apply to your life at any given moment.

The Minor Arcana

Despite their name, the Minor Arcana aren't minor or unimportant. They were likely added alongside the Major Arcana sometime in the fourteenth or fifteenth century to create the tarot deck we know today. This portion of tarot is believed to have been originally used for fortune-telling, and even individuals who were not considered high magicians could use them to perform divination.

The Minor Arcana consists of four suits of fourteen cards each: Wands, Pentacles, Swords, and Cups. Each suit contains four court cards (King, Queen, Knight, and Page) and ten number cards from Ace through Ten. The numbered cards are sometimes referred to as pip cards.

Everyday Guidance

The Minor Arcana cards can be extremely accurate in answering questions about the here and now, as they refer to specific areas of everyday life and human experience. They do not describe spiritual growth per se, but each of the areas to which these cards refer can certainly be incorporated into a pattern of spiritual development. You don't need to search for some deep mystical meaning to attach to them—sometimes what they are trying to tell you may be simple and easy to understand.

The Minor Arcana serve as an adjunct to the Major Arcana—a sort of commentary within the context of the reading. Their main function relates to elements of the everyday world, which exists for all of us no matter how spiritual we are. They show the everyday concerns, situations, challenges, and achievements you experience in your personal life. These are the cards that speak to your minor conflicts at work or with your parents, whereas the Major Arcana address your life's direction and passions.

When many (or all) of the cards in a reading come from the Minor Arcana, it's safe to say your future is in your own hands. Your decisions and actions will produce your future. You have the ability to set intentions and manifest your dreams.

THE REAL ROYALS: THE COURT CARDS

n most decks, each suit contains fourteen cards, including four court cards. Usually these cards are called the King, Queen, Knight, and Page, although some designers use labels such as Daughter, Son, Mother, and Father. The images on the court cards are usually illustrations of a King, a Queen, a Knight, and a Page. There may be some variation in costume or colors, depending upon the stylistic interpretation of the deck's creator. Sometimes the best way to differentiate the suit of the card is to note the symbol of the suit—cup, sword, wand, or pentacle—which is usually held by the person on the card.

The court cards are often seen as the most confusing cards in the deck because they can represent other people in the life of the individual for whom a reading is being done, or they may personify the individual. They can also be used as Significators, which will be explained in more detail later.

 TAROT TIP

Try assigning a court card to each of your friends and family members to help you discern the subtle variations in the energies of the cards and suits. For example, is your father gentle and kind as represented by the King of Cups, or is he rigid and stern like the King of Swords? What about your best friend: is she silly and childlike like the Page of Cups, or is she maternal and always baking cookies like the Queen of Cups? What about your boss? Matching important people in your life to their tarot counterpart can help you interpret your readings more fully.

King A king is a powerful ruler who exercises absolute authority over the territory he rules. He is, so to speak, at the top of the heap. Thus the King of any suit represents a completion point: there's no higher position to attain. A cycle that began with the Ace (the first card of the Minor Arcana) has been completed, and it's now time to either consolidate your position or begin a new cycle. The level of the King is where you release and let go, complete old tasks, and prepare for a new and more fulfilling way of life. An example of this could be someone who is super successful in their career, who's reached the pinnacle and made a lot of money, and who now decides that it's time to give back to the world. Bill Gates and Oprah are good examples of people signified by the King in tarot.

Queen

The Queen is a mature woman who is also a ruler in her own right; she's not just the King's consort. As such, she represents a woman or man who embodies and expresses the traditional feminine qualities of leadership, most importantly the qualities of creativity and cooperation. She has developed skills and wisdom that come only through years of experience. With the Queen, you achieve a level of maturity and self-confidence. You know when to compromise and when to take a firm stand. You are not intimidated by any situation. Yet you remain able to grow and evolve, and you can be flexible through understanding.

The Queen may portray a mature, capable person; an authority figure who is nurturing and understanding, or a mother image, sometimes your real mother. She has authority, just like the King, but utilizes her authority in the avenues of cooperation and nurturing instead of controlling and dominating. Beyoncé and Ellen DeGeneres are examples of powerful queenly individuals who use their nurturing qualities to express their authority.

Knight

A Knight is someone who has been singled out and honored by the ruler for having performed valuable services. A Knight takes on responsibility to the Crown he serves. At the level of the Knight you are fully aware of your path and your aims are clear. You want to get on with it in the most direct way possible, not waste time on irrelevancies. You feel an intense sense of dedication—to a project, an idea, a person. You've taken risks and gotten yourself together for the task at hand, and you are focusing your energies totally toward accomplishing your goal, to make the risk worthwhile. The Knight, who is often considered a messenger or an agent of movement, can refer to any gender. The message the Knight carries or the movement he suggests corresponds to the suit to which the card belongs. The Knight of Wands, for instance, might indicate a message about a creative project or a trip taken for fun and adventure.

Page The Page is a personal attendant of the royal family, like an errand boy or girl. It's his or her job to serve in order to advance. The Page represents preparing yourself to succeed at something. It involves being willing to assume a subordinate role—as younger people often do—and to learn about commitment. The Page is about challenging yourself, developing your inner resources, and taking something to a greater stage of accomplishment. You may experience some hesitancy, or feel that you are not fully prepared for the task, but you still hope the situation will turn out as you anticipate. For example, a freshman in college is a great example of a Page with the energy of just starting out on a new academic and social journey with many challenges ahead.

 TAROT TIP

The Page cards can represent either sex, and they usually refer to a young person or a child who is involved in the experiences related to the suit to which the Page belongs. Pages can indicate messengers, students/apprentices, youths, or young adults.

A Final Note about Court Cards

In addition to representing actual people in your life—family members, partners or lovers, friends, coworkers, neighbors, and so forth—the court cards can symbolize influences in your environment. They can also refer to situations, conditions, or characteristics of your life. Because our society today is more egalitarian than it was at the time tarot originated, it is possible to see a woman through a male card and vice versa. Here, feedback from the individual having cards read can help you to identify the person to whom a court card is referring.

Don't worry if you find court cards difficult to figure out at first. It takes time to learn when to trust your intuition and know that the card is referring to a person or a situation. When in doubt, describe the card both ways—you may find that it fits both a person and a situation.

ACE, TWO, THREE...: THE NUMBERED CARDS

Each suit also includes an Ace, which is considered to be the One card, followed by cards Two through Ten. Also known as pip cards, these combine the qualities of the suit with those of the number. Interpretations of the Minor Arcana vary according to the worldview and intentions of the deck's designer. Some tarot readers pay less attention to the Minor Arcana; others approach them from the perspective of numerology. In some decks, the pip cards do not display a scenario to suggest each card's meaning but simply show the corresponding number of the suit symbol. For example, the Three of Cups may simply depict three cups, without any storytelling imagery.

Although five hundred years' worth of tarot students and masters have produced some agreement on the meanings of the Minor Arcana cards, there is also a good deal of disagreement, and sometimes the pictures on the cards tell a different story than would be indicated by the combination of number and suit. The Eight of Cups in the Rider-Waite-Smith deck, for example, shows a man walking away from eight cups, which suggests leaving a relationship or emotional situation behind. However, the number eight connotes sincerity, abundance, and achievement, so drawing this card would seem to suggest success in matters of the heart. Therefore, you may prefer to base interpretations of the pip cards on the number rather than on any particular illustration—unless, of course, your intuition hooks into the picture and reveals something.

Chapter

2

GETTING STARTED: TAROT BASICS

FINDING A DECK THAT'S A GOOD FIT FOR YOU

Choosing a deck is a very personal process. With so many options to choose from, the decision boils down to your preferences and interests. The symbolism of each Major Arcana card is roughly the same in all decks, but it is depicted through different themes. You can find a deck for nearly any personal interest or spiritual path—what is most important is that you can easily understand the symbols and feel comfortable with them.

The fundamental layout of the cards themselves can influence your decision as well. For some people, the pictures on the Minor Arcana serve as memory aids to the cards' meanings…so for these individuals, cards depicting scenes will be important. Other readers prefer to dispense with storytelling scenarios on the Minor Arcana and are more comfortable with a simpler pip deck where cards like the Four of Wands will just have four wands in the image, not an elaborate scene of celebration. In some decks it's difficult to tell immediately if a pip card is upright or reversed; in others it's obvious.

Look at several decks and if one strikes your eye, try it out. Many stores keep sample packs available for you to examine and test before you buy, and a simple Internet search will turn up a myriad of choices. If you find a deck that is appealing, you can usually find a number of "unboxing" videos or reviews online that will give you a good taste of what the cards look like. Visiting popular social media sites will also expand your options, as a number of independent deck publishers promote their creations online. If you want to start out with a tried-and-true option, use the Rider-Waite-Smith deck, as most books about tarot are based on those illustrations.

If, after using a deck for a while, you do not feel entirely comfortable with it and its symbols, get another deck. Tarot readers often have several decks in their collections. Feeling an affinity for the deck you are using is essential. You need a deck that will resonate with your own inner symbology and that is compatible with your own belief system.

Therefore, if the symbols make you anxious or uncertain, try another deck. If you like the imagery—possibly crystals, animals, angels, herbs and flowers, or some abstract configuration—and if it seems to suit your personal point of view and you feel good using it, then you have found a good deck.

TAROT TIP

You can also let the universe guide you to your perfect deck. You might find an interesting deck while you're shopping for something completely different, or a friend might recommend one out of the blue. Sometimes the best decks are the ones found by chance.

Using More Than One Deck

Many people like to have two or more decks, sometimes for different purposes or to fit different moods or times of the year. For example, some individuals like to use one deck for practical readings and a different deck for spiritual readings. If you plan on reading for other people, some individuals prefer to keep one deck for their own spiritual development and use another deck for public readings. This way the energetic vibrations of your decks don't clash. These can be two identical decks or different designs, depending on your preference.

Handling Your Deck

Treat your deck as you would any precious possession of great value—with the utmost care and respect. Never leave it lying around unattended—you don't want negative energy to find its way to your deck. Always return it to its special place immediately after you have finished using it for practice, meditation, or a reading.

Clearing and Purifying the Cards

It is a good idea to clear your deck each time before you use it. When you get a new deck, you may want to do a short clearing ceremony before you use it for the first time in order to remove any previous energies or intentions the cards might be holding. This need not be complicated. Simply place the cards in front of you, hold your hands palms down over them, and say, silently or out loud, "I call upon the divine powers to clear and protect these cards, for my intention is to use them for good only. I declare that only good shall come from their use and that all negativity shall be turned away from them."

You can also use sacred smoke such as that from sage, palo santo, or incense to clear your deck. Simply run your deck through the smoke to cleanse it of any negative vibes. The simple act of knocking your deck three times is also helpful to remove any energies that have gathered in your deck.

THE SYMBOLISM OF THE SUITS

Regardless of what spin a particular artist chooses to put on his or her deck, a few things generally stay the same. Typically, there are four suits, for example, which make up the basic structure of the Minor Arcana. These suits correspond to the four elements, which are the building blocks of life; the vital and primal forces of the universe. These elements—Earth, Air, Fire, and Water—exist everywhere in our world, not only in a physical sense, but also as vibrations or energies. They are depicted not only in tarot, but also in the four primary tools magicians use, the four directions, the four seasons, the four Gospels in Christianity, and the Four Noble Truths in Buddhism.

Although it is easiest to recognize the suits in the Minor Arcana, you can find their presence on Major Arcana cards as well. The Magician, or Magus, for instance, is usually pictured with the symbols of all four suits before him, indicating his mastery of all the elements. The four suits may turn up on The World card, too, where they suggest a balance of these fundamental forces.

Wands

The suit of Wands corresponds to the element of Fire. Fire is active and outer-directed; linked with Spirit, will, self-expression, and inspiration. It suggests growth, expansion, and personal power. Because Fire represents archetypal masculine or yang energy, the symbolism used to depict this suit in tarot is distinctly phallic. Some decks use other images for the suit of Wands—rods, staves, clubs, branches sprouting leaves, lances, arrows, torches, or divining rods. Everyday Witch Tarot shows them as brooms.

Often the people on the Wands cards (in storytelling decks) are shown as warriors, heroes, leaders, or magicians—they are dynamic and creative people who charge forth into life with confidence and enthusiasm.

When Wands appear in a spread or reading, it's usually an indication that some sort of action or growth is possible. You might be heading off on an adventure of some kind or maybe you need to gather your courage to overcome a challenge. Perhaps you could benefit from using your intuition instead of logic to solve a problem. Maybe you need to have fun, take some risks, assert yourself, or be creative. A trip to the beach with your friends or a South American adventure with your partner may be in order.

Swords  The suit of Swords relates to the element of Air. Like Fire, Air is a masculine/yang force, so its symbol, too, is obviously phallic. Although usually depicted as a mighty battle sword, the suit's symbol may be represented by ordinary knives, athames (ritual daggers used by witches), scythes, axes, guns, or spears. Some swords are sturdy and functional, while others are ornate, reminiscent of King Arthur's Excalibur.

Storytelling decks frequently show the characters on the Swords cards as warriors, scholars, sages, teachers, or seekers—serious and thoughtful individuals who pursue answers to life's great questions. Often the images reveal suffering or hardship. That sense of loss and heartache is prevalent throughout this suit more so than any other suit in tarot. Although some cards in this suit have positive connotations, a number of them spell out difficulties in your path ahead.

When Swords turn up in a reading, it often means that mental or verbal activity is a priority. Perhaps you are studying or thinking too much, or, on the other hand, you might need to use your head and examine an issue clearly and rationally. The King of Swords, for instance, can advise you not to let your heart rule your head. Swords also represent communication, study, or cutting through murky situations with logic and good judgment.

Cups The suit of Cups is associated with the element of Water. Water's energy is receptive, inner-directed, and reflective; and is connected with the emotions, creativity, spirituality, and intuition. Because Water is a feminine or yin element, its symbols suggest the womb. In tarot, cups are usually shown as chalices or goblets, but any type of vessel can depict the nature of the suit. Some decks picture them as bowls, cauldrons, vases, urns, pitchers, coffee mugs, steins, baskets, or bottles. Regardless of the imagery, the principle is the same—cups represent the ability to receive and hold.

For the most part, the scenes that appear on these cards suggest comfort, security, and contentment. Because the suit of Cups symbolizes emotions, the people on the cards are usually shown in relationships of some kind—romantic, familial, friendship.

A reading that contains many Cups usually emphasizes emotions and/or relationships. Depending on the cards involved, you may be enjoying positive interactions with your friends or are seeking greater fulfillment in your dating life. Perhaps you are suffering a loss or disappointment, or are on your way to healing a broken heart.

TAROT TIP

Because Cups represent Water and its ability to be reflective and receptive, Cups can also describe a person who is intuitive, compassionate, sensitive, creative, or nurturing. All of these characteristics are traditionally feminine and relate to the inner reflections of a person and her emotional awareness.

Pentacles

Pentacles or pentagrams (five-pointed stars) correspond to the Earth element. Like Water, Earth is a feminine/yin force that energetically relates to our planet as the source of sustenance, security, and stability. The suit of Pentacles represents practical matters, money and resources, the body, and the material world. Tarot decks often portray the suit as coins or discs, but sometimes as shields, stones, rings, shells, crystals, wheels, stars, clocks, or loaves of bread. Regardless of the actual image used, the suit symbolizes physical resources, values, practical concerns, material goods, property, and forms of monetary exchange—things that sustain us on the earthly plane. Storytelling decks often depict people on the Pentacles cards engaged in some form of work or commerce, or enjoying the fruits of their labors and the things money can buy.

When Pentacles appear in a spread, it's a sign that financial or work-related matters are prominent in the mind of the person for whom the reading is being done. In some cases, these cards can also signify physical or health issues, or other situations involving the body or one's physical capabilities. The Queen of Pentacles, for example, can indicate a sensual woman who is at home in her body, who loves good food, creature comforts, and the finer things in life. Depending on the cards, this suit may suggest a need to focus on practical concerns. Or you could be too security conscious and putting emphasis on material things at the expense of spiritual, emotional, or intellectual considerations.

NUMEROLOGY BASICS

The numbers on the cards reflect stages of development and show how a matter is evolving. When interpreting the number cards of the Minor Arcana, consider the suit too; it will tell you the area of life to consider alongside the number. By combining the meanings of the suit and the number featured on a card, you can determine how the card applies to the particular situation for which the reading is being given. Basically, the characteristics of the suit plus the general meaning of the number equals a quick and easy definition of the Minor Arcana card.

Ace (One)

One signifies new beginnings or opportunities. It implies something coming into being, the starting point of a whole new cycle. It represents self-development, creativity, action, progress, a new chance, a rebirth.

The Ace shows that a seed has been planted, meaning that something has begun, though you may not yet know how it will develop. Aces symbolize potential growth. It's up to you to follow through—it won't automatically happen. The Ace indicates you have the choice to initiate something, that the time is ripe for new possibilities and growth.

The energy of One is solitary and self-contained. Drawing an Ace may indicate being alone or withdrawing into isolation to nurture a new idea, project, or experience before going public with it. Aces also can show focus, concentrated energy, and clarity of purpose.

 TAROT TIP

Barbara Moore, author of *The Gilded Tarot Companion*, calls an Ace "a gift from the universe." Aces symbolize a chance to start anew and realize possibilities and potential.

Two

The essence of Two is duality. This number depicts some kind of union or partnership, with another person, a spiritual entity, or two parts of yourself. Two also represents the balance of polarities, such as yin and yang, male and female, private and public, separate and together.

Two furthers the direction initiated with the Ace. It represents stabilizing and affirming the new opportunity. Sometimes Two shows a need to achieve balance with whatever new factor is being added to the situation that began with the Ace. Depending on the reading, the Two suggests either increased chances for a desirable outcome or greater obstacles involved in achieving that outcome. For example, if the Two of Cups came up in the future position in a relationship reading, it may suggest the possibility of a new romance, whereas if the Two of Swords was revealed, it could relate to a block that is preventing finding a new partner.

Two's vibration can indicate sensitivity to others, perhaps to the point where you consider their needs over your own. "Two-ness" can also mean a state of engaging yourself with another person or immersing yourself in an idea or project.

Three

We see the essence of Three expressed in the trinity of mind, body, and spirit. It is the number of self-expression, communication, expansion, openness, optimism, and clarity. With Three, you begin to see the big picture, understanding the details of how One and Two combine in your own process of growth and evolution. This is the point at which the project, idea, or relationship you initiated earlier begins to take form.

The number three represents movement, action, growth, and development, but in some cases expansion can happen too fast. You may scatter your energies or spread yourself too thin. There is a tendency to leap before you look, or to buy now and pay later. However, properly handled, Three's vibration is cheerful, optimistic, and pleasant, representing a period of happiness and benefits, so long as you pay attention to what you are doing.

Four

The number four equates with foundation. There are four elements, four directions, and four seasons, so four suggests totality, stability, and security. When Fours appear in a reading, it can indicate a time for self-discipline through work and service, productivity, organization, and pragmatism to establish a sound foundation.

Clarity is important now, so that you can work effectively to make your situation turn out positively. If you are in a place you want to be—a home, job, relationship—you might have to work to maintain stability; if you aren't where you want to be, drawing Fours suggests it's time to plan and work to make appropriate changes.

At this time, life can seem to be all work and no play, but sometimes that's necessary for you to accomplish your objectives. If your goals and purpose are clear, you won't mind doing the work, for you see the end result as beneficial. When Fours turn up in a reading, the message is to take slow, steady, determined steps and move patiently to bring your dreams to fruition.

Five

Five is the number of freedom, instability, and change. Its vibration is active, physical, impulsive, impatient, resourceful, curious, and playful. Drawing Fives in a reading suggests excitement, adventure, movement, and challenges might be ahead.

Sometimes Fives can be too much to handle, especially if you tend to be a quiet, sensitive person. The excitement and changes in your life may seem to be happening too fast, so that you feel you are caught in a whirlwind—or a hurricane. Thus Fives are often connected with stress and instability. You might need to slow down a bit and get some perspective before moving ahead. If an important decision is involved, "take five" before you make any commitment.

 TAROT TIP

Although Fives are an indication to go for it, consider the risks involved too. When Fives appear in a reading, you are willing to take risks because you love the excitement involved in the situation. The cards around the Five will indicate whether there is real danger or if things will work out to your advantage.

Six

Six is the number of service and social responsibility, caring, compassion, and community involvement. It signifies peace and quiet after the storm of Five. This is a time to keep it simple; practice self-care;

rest; and balance yourself and your surroundings. Any misunderstandings that occurred during an earlier period of upheaval can now be resolved harmoniously.

When Sixes appear in a reading, it's time to stop and catch your breath. You have created a comfortable pattern and can reap the rewards of your previous planning (Four) and risk-taking (Five). You feel centered and at ease with yourself and your circumstances. Unfavorable cards in the reading may indicate difficult circumstances yet to be faced, but Six cards rarely show anything negative themselves.

Six's vibration is cooperative; it can represent working with others or providing service of some kind. Just remember to take care of your own needs too. In some cases, Sixes in a reading can show a tendency toward solitary self-care—such as how spending time alone binge-watching your favorite shows can be cathartic after a period of intense activity or stress.

Seven

The number seven symbolizes the inner life, solitude, and soul-searching. Seven is a mystical number depicting wisdom and spirituality; there are seven heavens, seven days of the week (the seventh being holy), seven colors in the visible spectrum, seven notes in many musical scales, and seven major chakras.

When Sevens appear in a reading, they indicate a time of turning inward to discover the meaning of life, what has been happening to you, and why. You may be searching for answers. Perhaps you feel an intense need to be alone. Seven often refers to rebirth, religious inclinations, and spiritual resources. Some people retreat from the busyness of everyday life at this time to attend to their inner development. Emblematic of the path of solitude, analysis, and contemplation, Seven marks a time when you are exploring your individuality in your own way.

This is not a time to begin projects related to the material or financial world. Your energy is focused on the inner rather than the outer realm.

Now is a good time to examine your past experiences and evaluate what's happening in the present day. You might wish to study different spiritual outlets, take up tarot, or start paying attention to dreams—whatever will help you to find your own true path in life. In some cases, Sevens in the reading may indicate that you are spending too much time alone and need to socialize.

Eight

Eight represents abundance, material prosperity, and worldly power or influence. It is the number of leadership and authority. On the spiritual level, Eight symbolizes a universal consciousness; infinity's symbol is a figure eight turned on its side. This powerful number indicates you possess the organizational and managerial skills that contribute to material success—or that you need to develop them. If you have been devoting much of your time and energy to spiritual progress, the appearance of Eights in a reading says it's time to get your financial or other practical affairs in order.

 TAROT TIP

As the infinity glyph (also called a lemniscate) symbolizes wholeness, the number eight points to the development of multiple aspects of your life—physical, mental, and spiritual.

Eight's vibration is linked with honor, respect, equality, awards, public recognition, power, and abundance in all areas of life. When you draw Eights, the potential for achieving these benefits is likely, but sincerity and dedication are needed. You won't just luck into that desired promotion; it will be the result of all your long hours and hard work.

The Eight cards caution you to consider the welfare of others too. If there are unfavorable factors in the reading, you may need to be careful with money or possessions. Eights reversed (drawn upside down) can indicate that you have many issues around abundance—or the lack of it—yet to resolve.

Nine

The number nine represents universal compassion, tolerance for the many differences among different peoples, and the attainment of wisdom through experience. Drawing Nines suggests you have reached a level where you are comfortable dedicating your life to others' welfare, or to some worthy cause. The challenge is to avoid getting so caught up in the big picture—the greatest good for the greatest number—that you neglect what is closest to you.

Nine symbolizes integration and, in a reading, shows that you have established your life priorities—you know what you want and how you intend to get it. You understand the interaction between you and the world as a continuing process of living, being, moving. The Nine vibration allows you to see beyond the boundaries of the self into the totality of the universal. You are able to give freely of yourself because you feel complete within yourself.

The last single-digit number, nine represents the end of a cycle. It's time to tie up loose ends. In most cases, the Nine cards depict fulfillment, completion, wholeness, and the sense of satisfaction that comes from having reached a peak after a long, arduous climb.

Ten

Ten represents both an ending and a beginning, the point of transition from the completed cycle to the new cycle, which has not yet manifested. When Tens show up in a reading, whatever you have been working on or involved with is over. You've got whatever you are going to get out of it, and now it is time to bring in the new cycle that's been waiting in the wings.

This can be especially gratifying if you have been experiencing rocky times. If you have become complacent during a good period, drawing Tens tells you to challenge yourself and reach for a higher level. As a compound number, ten adds an extra dimension in a reading. Like ascending to a higher level of a spiral staircase, you can look down at precisely where you began and chart your progress. Now you have a choice to either stagnate in familiar and comfortable territory or take a chance and start something new and different.

As happens in any period of transition, you may feel unsure about making the decision to stay put or move on. You might feel you are sitting on the fence, with one foot on either side, not sure whether to jump all the way over. Sometimes it takes quite a while to get both feet on the same side of the fence. However, while you might have the luxury of postponing both decision and action for a little while, when Tens show up in a reading it's a signal that you need to make a decision.

NOT PURELY DECORATIVE: THE POWER OF COLORS

Many tarot decks display vivid and beautiful color palettes. But the colors shown on the cards are not purely decorative; they also embody specific symbolic, spiritual, psychological, and physiological properties. Colors can contribute to a certain design aesthetic, but they can also convey moods and messages as well.

In magical practice, colors correspond to the four elements. Red is associated with Fire, blue with Water, green with Earth, and yellow with Air. Because each suit is linked with an element, many tarot artists use the colors connected with the corresponding suits to trigger subconscious responses and insights. Therefore, some decks emphasize red on the cards in the suit of Wands, blue on the Cups cards, green on the Pentacles cards, and yellow on the Swords cards.

Studies show that people react psychologically and even physically to colors. For instance, red tends to make us feel stimulated, warmer, and can even raise pulse rate and body temperature slightly. Blue, conversely, calms and cools us. As you familiarize yourself with your tarot deck, notice how the artist has used colors to express certain qualities.

Many decks also use color to correspond with the chakra system. Red may be used to denote energies that relate to the root chakra and ideas of stability and grounding. Purple can symbolize the crown chakra and connection to the universe or the divine. The White Sage Tarot deliberately uses color associated with different chakras to add another dimension to readings.

 TAROT TIP

Early Christian paintings and stained-glass windows often show Jesus and Mary dressed in blue robes, which suggest serenity and compassion. We connect orange with fire, the sun, and warmth, while green represents growth, health, and in some countries, money.

THE UNIVERSAL SYMBOLISM

Symbols are a handy way to convey a lot of information and concepts in a quick way. However, they also embody the essence of whatever they stand for; they aren't merely a convenient form of shorthand. That's why they have such power, why they appear in diverse and widely separated cultures, and why they have endured for millennia.

Symbols that turn up again and again, in all parts of the world, possess universal appeal and resonate in what Swiss psychiatrist C.G. Jung called the collective unconscious. They mean essentially the same thing to everyone, regardless of age, race, religion, or nationality and get around the limitations of the rational, analytical left brain. Often we confront these symbols in dreams where they provide guidance and awaken us to parts of ourselves that we may have ignored in our waking lives. Tarot works in a similar manner.

TAROT TIP

Symbol is myth's vehicle, the chariot by which legend and story are drawn through the heart and mind and through time. Symbols express underlying patterns of thought and feeling stemming from the mythological roots that still affect people in a very real way.

The following table shows a number of common, universally understood symbols that you may notice on the cards in your tarot deck. They can be helpful keys as you examine the cards and learn their significances.

SYMBOL ◆	Meaning
BOOK ◆	Knowledge
BRIDGE ◆	Connection, harmony, overcoming difficulty
CIRCLE ◆	Wholeness, unity, protection, continuity
CROSS ◆	Union of male/female or earth/sky, integration
DOWNWARD TRIANGLE ◆	Divine feminine, Earth or Water elements
EGG ◆	Birth, fertility
FIVE-POINTED STAR ◆	Protection, the human body, physical incarnation
HORIZONTAL LINE ◆	Stability, earth, feminine energy
LANTERN ◆	Guidance, clarity, hope
MOON ◆	Secrets, intuition, emotions, feminine energy
MOUNTAIN ◆	Challenge, vision, achievement
OCEAN/WATER ◆	Emotions, the unknown depths of the psyche
RAINBOW ◆	Renewal, hope, happiness
ROSE ◆	Love
SIX-POINTED STAR ◆	Union of male/female or earth/sky, integration
SNAKE ◆	Transformation, hidden knowledge
SPIRAL ◆	Life energy, renewal, movement toward center
SQUARE ◆	Stability, equality, structure
STAR ◆	Hope, promise
SUN ◆	Clarity, vitality, optimism, contentment
TREE ◆	Knowledge, growth, protection, strength
TRIANGLE ◆	Trinity, three-dimensional existence, movement
UPWARD TRIANGLE ◆	Divine masculine, Fire or Air elements
VERTICAL LINE ◆	Movement, heaven, sky, masculine energy

When studying the symbolism in tarot, remember that your own responses and interpretations are what count most. Cars suggest movement and freedom to most people, but if you were in a serious car accident when you were young, cars may represent pain or danger to you. Trust your own instincts and intuition. After all, your tarot deck and your subconscious are attempting to communicate with you, and they will do it in imagery that you can understand.

ON A MORE PERSONAL LEVEL

Tarot decks can also contain their creators' personal symbols. These images may or may not mean the same thing to you as they do to their designers or to another person using the cards. Flexibility is part of what makes tarot so fascinating.

Perhaps the artist is attempting to get you to stretch your imagination by presenting you with new or atypical pictures. The noted and eclectic artist Salvador Dali repeats individual symbols such as a forked stick on some of the cards in his deck, as well as omitting or altering some familiar imagery entirely. The World card in his deck is anything but a pretty picture of joy, harmony, and abundance—possibly because the artist views our world as disturbing and never completely fathomable.

Tarot decks that come packaged with their own books or instructional guides generally explain the significance of the symbols displayed on the cards. Again, the images on most decks have some connection to the typical symbols discussed in this book. If your own feelings about the pictures on the cards don't coincide with the artist's, give your own responses precedence. You might also find that your interpretations of certain symbols change over time to reflect your spiritual growth.

Chapter

3

A PATH TO AWAKENING YOUR INTUITION

UNLOCKING YOUR PSYCHIC AWARENESS

Tarot can help you get more in touch with your inner self because it contains symbols and images that help you tap into your intuition and unlock the doors of your unconscious—bringing what is already inside to the surface for you to contemplate. This process helps you to form a connection with your higher self, or your essence. Many tarot scholars believe the Major Arcana was designed as a course in initiation to help individuals achieve a connection to their true higher nature, presented in twenty-two stages: the trump cards. But the Minor Arcana, too, is a rich body of information that you can use for personal development.

You could think of both sections of tarot as containing numerous chapters, one card being equal to a chapter. If you read these chapters in consecutive order, you'll notice a story unfolding. Each numbered card (the Major Arcana cards bear numbers too) evolves out of the previous one and develops into the following one. In this way, they convey information much as any other course or textbook might.

You can see this process for yourself by laying out the cards in order. First, take the Major Arcana and set them in front of you, zero through twenty-one. Can you see the story of The Fool's Journey start to unfold before your eyes? What happens after The Tower card spells destruction? You can do this with the Minor Arcana as well, placing each suit in order Ace through Ten. Which stories end on a happy note and which end in destruction? Whether or not you choose to study tarot in this linear fashion, however, is entirely up to you. There's no right or wrong way to seek truth.

STARTING SIMPLY: DAILY INSIGHTS

Perhaps the best way to learn tarot and start to gain confidence in your own perceptions is to practice with this tool every day. Each morning, you can shuffle your favorite deck, ask for guidance or what the general flavor of your day will be, and draw a single card. Sometimes this card will shed light on a problem, project, or issue you're dealing with in your life. Sometimes it may present the theme for the day. Or it may point to a matter you need to pay attention to.

On and off throughout the day, you can think about the card you drew that morning and how it relates to what unfolds during the day. Did you draw the Five of Wands and then experience an argument with a roommate or coworker? Do you have a meeting with your boss scheduled for a day you draw the Four of Wands? You can even place the card in a spot where you will see it often and reflect upon its meaning, letting its message guide you.

TAROT TIP

As you work on specific areas of your life, you'll see your growth reflected in the cards you draw. For instance, you might pick the Ace of Pentacles when you start a moneymaking venture. As the project bears fruit, you might draw the Seven of Pentacles, which shows you are beginning to see the results of your efforts.

It may appear that you're selecting cards entirely at random, but there's nothing arbitrary or chance about it. Your subconscious and/or your higher self are presenting information in this elegant way, and the cards you pick each day are never irrelevant.

This method of drawing a card a day can also help you to add to your personal definition of each card's meaning. Perhaps there is a day where you drew the Ace of Cups reversed (upside down), and then you ended up spilling your morning coffee on your favorite sweater. Now you know to be more cautious (or perhaps choose a less desirable outfit) the next time the Ace of Cups reversed comes up.

Sometimes you might find yourself drawing the same card over and over again across a span of a week, a month, or more. Like a recurring dream, these "stalker" cards suggest there is a major theme in your life that you need to take a closer look at. Don't discount these cards—instead pay closer attention; they speak of an important message that you need to be mindful of.

GROWING THROUGH THE MAJOR ARCANA

The Major Arcana are one of the greatest tools for spiritual and personal growth. The powerful images on these cards portray archetypes that exist within the collective unconscious and that connect you to something larger than yourself. At the spiritual level, each of the Major Arcana cards represents a state of being or an inner truth about yourself.

The simplest way to understand the Major Arcana in spiritual terms is to think of it as an ascending staircase with twenty-two steps. Each card represents a lesson you must learn in order to move up to the next step. And you have to figure out how to do this yourself; there is no set system.

You can either study the trump cards in consecutive order, or choose individual cards that represent areas or concepts you wish to work on, in whatever order suits your purposes. Or separate the Major Arcana from the entire deck, shuffle, and draw a card for study, letting your inner knowing guide you. Whatever you choose, you will find that it is the right path for you.

If, for example, you wish to discover the source of inner strength, pick the Strength card. Start by simply gazing at the card, without analyzing it. Let the colors, pictures, and symbols connect with your intuition and reveal themselves to you gradually, before you begin to examine the images more carefully.

TAROT TIP

You can recite this if you want to practice meditating on tarot with affirmations: "Everything that I believe to be true about the universe, I understand is also true about myself. Its Goodness is my goodness. Its Power is my power. Its Presence in me is my true self. There is only one True Self."

In her companion book to the Sacred Circle Tarot deck, Anna Franklin suggests you approach the card as if you were going to enter it, like walking through a doorway, and interact with the scenario depicted there. Don't just see the images—experience them. Allow your senses to come into play. Feel the sun on your face, the grass under your feet. Witness the murkiness and mystery connected with The Moon or the burning sensation of anger, jealousy, obsession, and fear depicted by The Devil. Have fun with this exercise and see what the characters in the card reveal to you. What would you say to The Empress if she was sitting right in front of you?

One of the best ways to really understand a card is to have an intimate association with it. This exercise will provide you with insights and knowledge that no book or individual can hope to bestow on you. To really get to know each card, you need to step inside it and experience the energy that is inherent in the images.

Write down what you glean from your study—your insights, awarenesses, questions, impressions, and feelings. Notice how the energies represented by the cards are playing out in your own life—or how you would like to be able to express them. Because the trump cards are quite complex, it's probably best to limit your study to one card at a time, until you understand it—even if it takes several days or weeks.

USING THE MINOR ARCANA TO GET EVERYDAY ADVICE

The cards in the Minor Arcana represent everyday concerns and earthly matters—those mundane tasks and encounters that you run into as part of your daily living. As discussed earlier, the suit of Cups represents the emotions and relationships; Pentacles stand for financial and physical conditions; Swords symbolize mental issues and communication; and Wands are linked with creativity, spiritual considerations, and willpower.

Working On a Specific Issue

A great way to really get to know the Minor Arcana is to first determine which suit covers an issue or situation you want to work on right now. Then pick the card within that suit that speaks most directly to what you want to accomplish. For instance, if your goal is to rekindle the love and affection in a romantic relationship, select the Six of Cups from your deck.

Begin by gazing at the card for a minute or two, without attempting to analyze it. Just let the colors, symbols, and so on impress themselves on your subconscious. Pay attention to any thoughts, feelings, or insights that arise into your awareness and write them down if you like.

Next, examine the card more closely. Contemplate the symbols depicted on the card to ascertain their meanings. In most storytelling decks, for example, the Six of Cups shows a young man and woman (sometimes a male and a female child) in a pleasant setting—a peaceful village, or a sunny meadow in the country. Their youth is one of the keys to understanding the card—innocence and openness are necessary for love to flourish. The colors are cheerful and bright, signifying optimism. The image is one of generosity, comfort, companionship, and joy. Often the six cups pictured on the card are filled with flowers, a familiar symbol of love. Sometimes the male is portrayed offering one of the cups to the female as a token of affection, which indicates that sharing, giving of oneself, and being receptive—give and take—are essential in any partnership.

What symbols do you see on your own card? Some decks are more symbol-rich than others. What individual and universal meanings do they hold? It may help to make a list of the symbols you notice and your interpretations of them. Continue studying the card you've selected until you've uncovered all the information you feel is relevant at this time. After a day or two, revisit the same card to see if you receive additional insights from it. If you own more than one deck, examine the same card in each deck. One card may reveal something that was not apparent in another.

This exercise and others like it will help you to build your own personal relationship to both your deck of cards and the meaning behind each image. Do not let standard definitions confine you as you explore what each of these cards means to you.

 TAROT TIP

It might be helpful to keep a tarot journal to record which cards you get and how you react to them. Each person's responses will be different—and your own responses will vary from day to day—so simply jot down whatever comes to you without censoring yourself, even if it doesn't make sense immediately. We'll discuss journaling more later in this chapter.

DEVELOP AND TRUST YOUR INTUITION

Your sixth sense is part of who you are—it isn't something spooky or otherwise otherworldly. Everyone on this planet (and likely other planets too) has intuition; some just know how to use it more fully than others. Your intuition is a skill that can be developed and honed. Like the muscles in your body, your psychic center needs to be utilized and exercised on a regular basis.

A myriad of factors—such as your moods, intelligence, education, interests, health, state of mind, past experiences, future aims, ability to be open to experiences, and the time of day and setting—can all affect how your intuition performs. Certain individuals even believe that whether or not you are menstruating (if you are a woman) can play a role in the sensitivity of your psychic ability. You will find that some people are naturally more intuitive than others—psychic ability is like any other skill—but that does not mean you cannot be just as good as someone else. You will never know unless you try!

How long it will take you to develop this muscle is up to you. A lot depends on your personal goals, the quality and length of time you invest, individual aptitude, and factors as yet unknown. Sometimes people work diligently for a long time and nothing seems to be happening, and then, bingo!—a portal appears. It's like walking along a dull, dreary street and suddenly passing through a gate into a beautiful, flower-filled courtyard hidden behind the facade of a building. For others, it may be a slow and steady progression toward their ultimate goal.

As you learn to trust your psychic responses and let them operate on their own, success becomes automatic. You'll wonder how you ever got along without this valuable skill!

Using Tarot to Improve Intuition

There are many ways to discover your own inner knowing. One of the best of these is the contemplation of symbols, and you are lucky because tarot is full of symbols. Symbols speak directly to the unconscious. Thinking about the cards' symbols awakens the corresponding information in the unconscious, and that in turn allows you to tap into your intuition, to see the truth in the heart of the matter. By reflecting on the deep meanings of the symbols on a regular basis, you set in motion an inward process that will reveal inner truths about yourself and enable you to look outward.

Once you start paying attention to symbols, you will see them everywhere, from the logo on the car in front of you during rush hour to the way two sticks make a pattern on the sidewalk. Each of these symbols has its own energy and meaning, and you can use this to help you understand and tap into your intuition.

Other Ways to Develop Intuition

Trust and awareness are essential to developing your intuition. If you are not accustomed to consciously paying attention to your thoughts and feelings, it may take a bit of time for you to get used to doing so. The important thing is to make a commitment and follow through on it. Don't expect immediate success, but don't rule it out either. Intuition is very subtle, and as a general rule most of us have not been taught to recognize and know when we are receiving information. It will take a little time and patience, but you will soon learn that your intuition has been there all along…you have just been focusing on what's on your phone instead of the images playing out in your own mind.

 TAROT TIP

If you want to build your predictive skills, try using the cards to predict the outcome of something that you will know tomorrow, such as the winner of a sporting event or a political election. Keep track of your hits. Over time, your success rate will likely improve.

Notice coincidences and pay attention to signs. If you observe or experience something out of the ordinary, or with unusual frequency, take note of it. See if it ties into anything else. If any thoughts pop into your head in conjunction with the sign or coincidence, pay attention to them too. These subtle experiences will really help you understand how the psychic process works.

 TAROT TIP

Using your cards regularly and trusting what they reveal to you, paying attention to your impressions, and noting how the information you receive from the cards plays out in your life will strengthen your psychic "muscles." In time, your intuition will be automatically activated when you lay out your cards for a reading.

Meditation can also help you become aware of the thoughts and impressions you receive from your intuition. During meditation, you empty your mind and allow it to be filled by something other than everyday, rational thinking. You relax into a calm state and invite input from your higher self, subconscious, angels, guides, god, goddess, or whatever term you choose to use. Stilling the mind is easier said than done, however. Some people focus on their breathing, some listen to music, some chant or repeat mantras to quiet their minds. You can also gaze at a meaningful symbol, such as a mandala or a tarot card. The objective is to keep your mind and heart open, and to allow insight to flow into your awareness rather than permitting your thoughts to jump about.

CONNECTING TO THE UNKNOWN

Meditating on the cards activates your unconscious repository of images, those symbols and pictures that have been stored in your mind over the years, and these can be used for spiritual progress. If you choose to use it as a spiritual tool, working with tarot can open a passageway between the material and the spiritual realms. The cards offer a way to connect with that which cannot be seen or touched.

You will find that using tarot over a period of time will open you up to a greater awareness of your own spiritual nature and a deeper knowledge of your spiritual self. You can use tarot to connect you to the world beyond this one, to pull back the veil that exists between this one and the next.

Many tarot readers use the cards to communicate with entities that are not on this plane—spirit guides, deceased loved ones, ghosts, and other life-forms. Tarot is a tool that, if you choose, can assist you in learning more about what exists beyond the physical realm. Of course, you do not *have* to use the cards in this fashion. Whether you choose to communicate and connect with your spiritual nature or entities beyond the known is up to you. The cards are in your hand and you wield the power.

 TAROT TIP

If you are using tarot for spiritual development, keep a deck for this purpose only. Don't let anyone else touch this deck. It can be identical to the deck you use for readings or a different design entirely. What's important is that the images on the cards speak to your higher consciousness.

TRACK YOUR JOURNEY WITH A JOURNAL

As you study tarot, it's a good idea to keep a journal. You can choose from a variety of options, from a fancy notebook to a document on your computer or notes on your phone—choose what works best for you. This is your place to put into words your personal definitions of each card, explore your journey and spiritual development, and even explore your own creativity.

A simple way to start is to write the name of a card at the top of each page. Each time you examine the card, date your entry. Write down all the thoughts and impressions you experience when you work with the card. Watch your definitions change and evolve over time.

If you are doing readings, sketch the spread you've used and label each card. (Spreads are explained and demonstrated later in the book.) Add comments about your state of mind, situations in your life, or anything else that you feel may be relevant. You can then revisit your readings at a later time. Make sure to write about whether your prediction came true or any insights that came to you.

Once you have a journal devoted to your study of tarot, make a covenant with your tarot journal—that means to put into words "why" you are studying tarot and what you want to get out of this exercise. Do you want to tell the future or gain a deeper understanding of your subconscious? Study what you have written for a few minutes and see if you are satisfied with your purpose. You may want to make changes.

Your statement of purpose might go something like this:

I'm keeping my tarot journal for the purpose of getting in touch with my higher self and discovering my intuition. My goal is to use tarot to guide me in making decisions that will lead me to my true happiness and purpose in life. I believe keeping this journal will help me to grow my mind, strengthen my body, and bring power to my spirit.

You are making this agreement with yourself, and it is up to you to keep to the terms you make. Trust your inner self to keep its part of the bargain.

Chapter

4

INTERPRETING THE MAJOR ARCANA

INTRODUCTION TO THE TRUMP CARDS

The Major Arcana are the iconic cards of tarot, and the images are usually detailed and highly significant. This is where we find The Devil that startles us and The Star that draws us in. These cards as a whole represent spiritual or universal forces, higher consciousness, the collective, and archetypes—these are the big dogs of tarot. When they turn up in a spread, they could be considered messages from the divine or your spirit guide trying to get your attention. This may indicate that you are being helped or influenced by powers beyond your own everyday awareness, or that aspects of the reading (or the subject of the reading) have implications beyond the obvious, physical ones—even beyond your own personal existence. This is karma- and life lesson–level information. A spread with many trumps in it shows that the matter is complex and involves issues of a broader nature. It can suggest that to handle the issue, you need to ask for assistance from a higher power and trust that power to guide you.

Some people view the trumps as indicators that fate or destiny is involved with the subject of the reading. To other readers, the presence of Major Arcana cards means you are seeing the results of past actions starting to manifest in your life.

Where the Cards Fall in a Spread

Once you learn about spreads, you'll see how the position of the cards is also important. That's especially true of the Major Arcana cards. Do they appear in the early or past portion of a spread or toward the end or future part? Do they represent opportunities or obstacles? Do they show areas you are aware of or hidden influences? Whenever a trump card turns up in a spread, pay extra attention to it, for it can reveal a great deal.

Importance of Reversed Cards

You will notice as you do readings that shuffling the cards can cause some of them to get turned upside down. When cards appear upside down in a spread, they are said to be reversed. Some readers simply turn reversed cards upright again. Others interpret cards differently when they are reversed than when they are upright.

People disagree about the significance of reversed cards. Many tarot readers consider a reversed card to be weakened, so that it has less impact than it would if it were upright. You may also choose to say that the energy of that card is "blocked" and cannot fully manifest. Another popular view suggests that reversed cards depict more negative, dark, or malevolent energies at work. Reversals encourage us to see beyond and through the obvious, and to consider a matter's underlying dynamics as well as its apparent ones.

When coming up with your own interpretations for each of the seventy-eight cards, choose first whether you want to read reversed cards or not. There is nothing better or worse about choosing one option over the other. Many respected tarot authorities do not read with reversed cards. Next, decide what each reversed card means for you. You do not need to stick with the same technique for interpreting reversed cards or keep the definition static for every situation. For example, The Tower reversed could be a time of rebuilding while The Chariot reversed may mean that you are being blocked from moving forward. Use your intuition to decide which option is best for you.

Whether you choose to interpret reversed cards in a spread or read only upright positions is up to you. You may wish to work with tarot for a while before you decide whether to interpret reversals in a different manner, and if so, how.

THE FOOL

THE FOOL is a fascinating figure, yet he can be an ambiguous symbol. Related to the joker of the ordinary playing deck, which is often used as the wild card, The Fool seems beyond ordinary cares and concerns. In many tarot decks, The Fool is shown standing on the edge of a cliff, about to step off into thin air, yet he gazes upward as if he expects the heavens to support him. He is unconcerned—or unaware—of any danger lying ahead.

Like a drifter, he usually carries all his worldly possessions tied in a small bag on a stick over his shoulder. He may carry a rose—the symbol of love—or a traveler's staff. Often he is dressed in bright colors, and the card's general impression is cheerful and sunny. In some decks he is accompanied by a dog, which symbolizes natural instincts. The dog plays around The Fool, sometimes pulling him back from the danger ahead, suggesting that our instincts, if followed, provide us with guidance on our life journeys.

Ordinarily, The Fool is shown as a person full of confidence—often the confidence of youth—and trust in the universe. He symbolizes that blind leap of faith that we all must take upon entering the journey of life itself.

❧ Interpretation

When The Fool appears in a reading, it symbolizes embarking on a new way of life. This may involve a physical journey, moving to a new place, starting a new job, or getting married or divorced. Often the appearance of The Fool indicates a person who is beginning a spiritual path and has absolute faith in the universe. In such a case, the person has no fear and feels that everything will turn out well. The person may be in touch with the intuitive realm, or may simply be naive about the future. The Fool represents a state of openness and faith that she'll be supported in her adventure.

In mythology, The Fool is linked to Dionysus, the early Greek god of theater, wine, and special religious events. In medieval courts, the king's fool, or jester, was given license to make fun of everything and everybody with no threat of punishment. His was a special role in a time when simpletons, or fools, were believed to possess divine madness, and irrational behavior was thought to be the result of possession by a god or spirit. The Fool is also associated with the Green Man of the Celtic tradition, a god of fertility and nature's ability to restore itself.

Upright

At this time, you are out of sync with the rest of the world, but in a positive way. You may want to go out on your own, full speed ahead. Or you may feel isolated from the group, a loner. Your experience of the current situation is different from those around you—you feel as if you are marching to a different drummer, and you probably are. Listen to that drummer, for this is the beat of your authentic self, trying to get your attention.

Reversed

The time for independent action may not be right. You must discriminate between your dreams—of going off on an adventure or leaving everything behind—and reality. The advice "Don't quit your day job" may apply here: this is not to say that what you want to do is invalid, only that you must consider all of the pros and cons carefully.

THE MAGICIAN

THE MAGICIAN represents wisdom and the power to control unseen forces that operate in human lives. A deeply complex symbol, he is usually depicted as a male figure with the traditional magician's tools, which are also the symbols of the Minor Arcana suits: pentacles, swords, cups, and wands.

Traditionally, The Magician holds a wand aloft in one hand toward the heavens and divine power, while his other hand points downward to the earth. Above his head may float the symbol for infinity. He knows how to use his tools to connect the two worlds. In some decks a garden of roses, lilies, and greenery (representing the plant kingdom) may lie at his feet.

These symbols tell us that The Magician is able to manipulate the material world by aligning it with the spiritual plane to manifest certain outcomes.

✵ Interpretation

The appearance of The Magician in a reading indicates latent powers that have not yet manifested. This card suggests that everything in the universe is available before us, and if we learn to use energy correctly we can manifest the results we desire. It is the task of The Magician to handle energy well, to manipulate and control it for beneficent purposes.

The Magician shows us that what we consider to be illusion is another form of reality, and what we consider to be reality can be mere illusion. This is not trickery, but rather a deep understanding of how we must learn to use our intellect, intuition, and practical skills to differentiate between the two worlds.

The Magician is a card of power, because it refers to how each of us creates our own universe. This card suggests that we have the ability to control our own lives, that we can set intentions to achieve our goals—so long as we go about it the right way and for the right ends.

This card is primarily about self-development; as the number one card in the Major Arcana, it marks the beginning of the road to spiritual enlightenment. We are able to control our universes, but in order to do so, we must learn how to reach our goals, whether they are spiritual or mundane.

Mythologically, The Magician corresponds to Hermes, Greek messenger of the gods and guide of souls in the underworld. He has the ability to communicate between the celestial and earthly realms. As a guide, he mediates between our conscious daylight world and the unconscious, hidden recesses of the psyche, often in dreams. The Magician suggests the use of higher intuitive forces, which may appear as a flash of insight. He can serve as an inner guide who, if we listen carefully, will prompt us to develop our potential.

Upright

This signifies new beginnings and new choices. It indicates someone who is willing and able to manipulate a situation to achieve a goal. It suggests leadership potential, ambition, desire for action, and new relationships coming into being. The tools for whatever you desire are already at hand, as is the knowledge for using them correctly—evaluate them and use them properly.

Reversed

Now is not the time for change. Maybe you are not ready internally or are not fully prepared in a practical or logistical way. You need to be patient, and the situation will work out properly. You may be experiencing self-doubt about a new venture, or your energy levels may be too low to accomplish your aims. There is no sense in rushing things prematurely. Wait until the time is right.

TAROT TIP

The Magician's costume varies stylistically with different decks, but he usually wears a belt. In the Rider-Waite-Smith deck, his belt is the ouroboros, or snake biting its tail—an alchemical symbol for wholeness. This represents the power to heal through connecting the two worlds within one's self.

THE HIGH PRIESTESS

THE HIGH PRIESTESS is a most mysterious card, representing secret knowledge. She symbolizes feminine spiritual power, or the goddess from whom all life comes and to whom all returns.

In many decks, she is depicted as a serene-faced female figure, sometimes seated with a book on her lap. This book represents the Akashic Records, the divine repository of human lives past, present, and future. Sometimes she is standing, holding a staff and pointing toward an unseen object in the distance, an indication of something yet to be revealed.

She sometimes sits or stands between two pillars, which represent the dual nature of our world: good and evil, light and dark, positive and negative. She promises reconciliation of these opposites to those willing to follow the spiritual path of understanding universal law. Occasionally, The High Priestess is depicted sitting at the doorway to a temple, as if welcoming students to enter and learn her secrets. A crescent moon at her feet may warn of the danger of releasing higher knowledge to those unprepared to handle it.

On her breast, The High Priestess usually wears a cross, symbolic of the four elements—Fire, Earth, Air, and Water—held in balance. She may wear a crown depicting the three lunar phases that symbolize the three stages of womanhood: maiden, mother, crone. This particular card is reminiscent of the Egyptian mother goddess Hathor, who wears a similar headdress.

❋ Interpretation

When The High Priestess appears, she indicates that something hidden, or within you, is preparing to come forth, or that you need to pay more attention to your inner world of dreams, imagination, and intuition. Usually, you know the importance of developing this part of your life, but you may have been holding back out of fear or lack of motivation.

The High Priestess may also indicate that you are attempting to hide something that needs to be revealed. The High Priestess represents our potentials that have yet to be discovered and manifested—our secret selves longing to be recognized.

The High Priestess is linked to the Egyptian goddess Isis, queen of the intellect, in her veiled form. Isis fully understands the workings of the universe and is familiar with both the upper world and the underworld, where her husband Osiris reigns. She knows the secrets of regeneration after death, and of the transformative powers inherent in secret knowledge.

Upright

You are experiencing awareness of the invisible world, where inner change takes place before it manifests in the outer, material world. Your attunement to these inner, invisible sources is acute now, and you are in a position to take advantage of this. You may want to practice meditation to go deeper into your inner core. Tune in to your inner voice and spiritual awareness by whatever meditative method works for you (visualization, guided, following breath, and so on).

Reversed

Something within you is seeking recognition. You may have been neglecting your true purpose, although at a deep level you are aware that motivation is stirring to make a change. You may be keeping this situation private for now, not wanting others to know about it. Those around you may notice that you seem vague or not quite yourself. That's okay—ignore them. You are in the process of manifesting spiritual fulfillment and well-being.

THE EMPRESS

THE EMPRESS is a card of beauty and creativity, the matriarch incarnate, symbolic of the Universal Mother. She represents the feminine in maternal roles: procreation, nurturing, the security and comforts of home, and domestic harmony.

The Empress is a mature female figure, often seated on a throne. In some decks she is shown standing in a field, surrounded by flowers and vegetation representative of Mother Nature and her harvest. Full-breasted and sometimes pregnant, she symbolizes fruitfulness and abundance.

As a symbol of The Empress's royal position, she sometimes holds a scepter and wears a crown. In many decks, a shield or coat of arms leans against her throne.

❋ Interpretation

When The Empress appears, a strong feminine energy is at work. As both a mother figure and representative of the traditional female role, The Empress is a creative force that works for harmony. She brings disparate things together, reconciling differences, like a person running a household must do. This is a card of emotional control and congeniality.

The Empress also refers to the person's emotional and physical resources—for nurturing, healing, feeding, and supporting other people. Often there is a situation in the person's life where love and nurturing are required—sometimes by the person herself, sometimes by others. This card may refer to the way the person was mothered, for the first and most significant relationship you form is with your mother, and this relationship has a direct bearing on all subsequent relationships.

The Empress is linked to all of the mother goddesses of antiquity, but especially to Greek Hera, the wife of Zeus and the quintessential matriarchal figure. (She is called Juno by the Romans.) As a primary symbol for feminine fertility, she is associated not only with Demeter, Ceres, and all the pagan mother goddesses, but also with the Christian Virgin Mary.

Upright

You are in a position of nurturing someone else or several others. You could be caring for children or the sick, or being supportive of a spouse or friend in need. This card could also refer to a pregnancy, or the desire for a pregnancy. It is appropriate for you to be nurturing now, for you have the inner strength and the ability to do so without depleting yourself.

Reversed

It's time to nurture yourself. You may have been spending too much time caring for others (or you may have recently had a child whose demands have worn you out). You need to take time out for yourself instead of neglecting your own needs. This is a call for self-love, balance, and the awareness that you deserve the same care and attention you give to your loved ones.

TAROT TIP

As a female authority, The Empress may signify, depending on her place in the spread, the person's need to become a female authority, especially if the person is a woman. In a man's reading, she indicates that he needs to recognize the feminine component of himself and acknowledge its power to unite opposing forces.

IV

THE EMPEROR

THE EMPEROR is a figure of supreme authority, as his title suggests. He is usually shown seated on a throne, sometimes flanked by animals. In some decks these are ram's heads, symbolic of masculine power. He often wears robes over a full suit of armor, holds a scepter in the shape of the Egyptian ankh, and is crowned elaborately. In some decks his shield, bearing the symbol of the imperial eagle, leans against the throne. He is clearly a figure to be reckoned with. Often he appears outdoors, against a backdrop of mountains, another reference to worldly power. His age and position of authority speak of experience and wisdom gained. Although he is depicted as a warrior, his attitude is one of a kind ruler.

While at rest, The Emperor's attitude suggests he is willing to fight for what is right and what is his duty to protect. He is the executive, or leader, who has reached the summit of authority and achieved worldly power. He is the builder in the material world who strives to make constructions of lasting value and importance. Thus The Emperor is a traditional father figure, who lays down the ideals, morals, and aspirations for the entire family to follow.

Interpretation

When The Emperor appears in a reading, look for issues related to authority. Although The Emperor represents worldly power and wisdom, he is not simply a figure who gives commands to others. He understands that peace requires a willingness and ability to defend it.

The Emperor teaches the meaning of power and how to use it in this world. Though not overtly aggressive, he tells us that it is necessary sometimes to take up "arms" against evil forces. As a protective male

---

TAROT TIP

The Emperor is related to Zeus, the father god of the Greek pantheon. The Romans called him Jupiter; the Norse called him Thor. All these deities were known for throwing thunderbolts or lightning. In some decks The Emperor carries lightning instead of the ankh.

force, especially of the home and of domestic harmony, he personifies the ideal that what is worth having is worth fighting for.

The Emperor in a reading can also indicate issues concerning the biological father, or authority figures in general. The time has arrived to become the authority figure, rather than depending on others to provide protection. The Emperor often appears when the person is struggling to achieve independence, become his own person, and reconcile father issues.

When The Emperor appears, the individual's real father may have recently died or may die soon, a situation that can bring up feelings of being abandoned by a protective father figure. It's also possible that someone in the person's life is acting as a father figure, perhaps a boss or a husband. Whether this is positive or negative will be indicated by the placement of the card in the layout.

From a pagan perspective, The Emperor represents the Horned God who accompanied the Great Mother Goddess. As consort to The Empress, he symbolizes parenthood and masculine creativity.

Upright

This indicates that you are involved with the established order, or with someone who represents the establishment. You may have a need to identify with a powerful group—religious, ideological, intellectual, economic, or political—and to be one of them. Or you may be associating with someone else who has this need.

Reversed

You may be in conflict with the established order—at your job or with your family, religion, or ethnic group. Perhaps you feel pressured to accept responsibilities you don't want or don't feel capable of handling. You may have recently experienced a loss of power, or you may lack the energy required to reach your goals. A need for more experience, drive, or improved health could be indicated.

THE HIEROPHANT

THE HIEROPHANT is a figure with authority and power, like The Emperor, but whereas The Emperor's power is secular, The Hierophant's power is of a spiritual nature. Often he is shown as a religious leader. Some decks title him The Pope. He is usually seen seated on a throne, dressed in priestly raiment, crowned, and holding a scepter. His implements will vary according to the theme of the deck.

His scepter symbolizes the three worlds—the physical, the astral, and the etheric. His free hand is usually held aloft in a position of blessing. Acolytes may stand before him, deferring to his wisdom and understanding as a representative of authority. He contains within himself the wisdom of a spiritual calling, and like The High Priestess, The Hierophant frequently sits or stands between two pillars, which signify the duality of matter and spirit.

In this role, The Hierophant is responsible for making spiritual decisions for others and for blessing them. Some decks show two crossed keys below him, representing the intellect and intuition. Unlike The High Priestess, whose world is internal and ephemeral, The Hierophant's influence, though of a spiritual nature, is of this world, achieved through conscious choices made on an intellectual basis.

❋ Interpretation

The Hierophant suggests that the person has chosen a religion or philosophy by which to guide his or her life. Sometimes the card indicates a need to disentangle yourself from such an association.

The Hierophant symbolizes any organized institution—be it religious, philosophical, educational, spiritual, or temporal—that exerts authority over its followers or participants, a kind of mind control. Such groups often insist that their way is the only way, that theirs is the ultimate truth.

When The Hierophant appears, a choice is being presented. At this stage of your spiritual development, you are challenged to remain a follower or to break out and find your own individual path. The Hierophant asks whether you will continue to depend on an outside authority, or will you learn to think for yourself? The answer is yours alone, but what you decide will affect the rest of your life.

The Hierophant is linked in myth to the centaur Chiron, teacher of Apollo, the god of truth and healing. Half man, half horse, the centaur represents the quest for meaning in life. The centaur is a teacher figure who guides the spiritual seeker to find a connection or bridge between the two worlds—the inner and outer, the material and spiritual. The Hierophant's understanding goes beyond organized religion and is based on the truth that is found inside all of us.

Upright

Upright, this card tells you that an authority is active in your life, whether it is in a religious, philosophical, social, or other capacity. You feel a great deal of loyalty to this tradition or group and choose to live in accordance with the beliefs you share with it. You may aspire to become a leader, or you may have a close relationship with the leader. There may also be a judgmental quality involved. Sometimes this card can suggest challenges or limitations of a spiritual nature.

Reversed

You may wish to overthrow an old tradition—religious, ideological, intellectual, or cultural—that you feel is suffocating you or that simply no longer serves your needs. You can choose to live by whatever philosophy resonates with your true nature. You want to direct your actions your own way, even if this puts you in conflict with some established tradition or one you were raised to believe. Perhaps your faith is being challenged in some way and you must reevaluate beliefs you've always taken for granted.

TAROT TIP

As a spiritual teacher whose task is to connect the world of humans with that of the gods, to forge a link between the material and spiritual worlds, The Hierophant is a pontifex, an ancient word that meant maker of bridges, and that is used to designate a priest.

THE LOVERS

THE LOVERS card often shows a young couple with an angel-like figure hovering above them. The angel's wings are spread out over them, and its hands are held above their heads in a gesture of blessing. Traditional decks depict them as Adam and Eve, standing respectively before the Tree of Eternal Life and the Tree of the Knowledge of Good and Evil. Imagery in other decks suggests choice is involved as well as the possibility of union.

Some decks include three people, indicating that the third party—who might be another young person or an older parental figure—was an influence in the couple's relationship. In decks where three figures are shown, a winged, cupid-like figure on a cloud may appear and point an arrow in the direction of one of the women.

Interpretation

Although many readers interpret this card as representing romantic love, it is allegorically a statement about a union of opposites, whether between two people or within ourselves. The Lovers refers to thoughtfulness in making choices. The male and female figures are symbols not only of human love but also of the dual nature within ourselves. We all have opposing traits and inner dichotomies that need to be reconciled. Partners often experience conflict that requires making choices.

When The Lovers card appears, it points to the need to heal a rift. Although it can herald a romantic involvement, it most often turns up when a critical life decision must be made, sometimes in connection with a love relationship. This card suggests that you are at a crossroads.

TAROT TIP

In decks that show one young man and two young women on The Lovers card, the implication is that he must choose between them, another indication that this card is as much about choice as it is about partnership.

You have to consider all of the ramifications of the situation and choose carefully to further your own development and to accommodate the needs of others in the situation.

In mythology, The Lovers card reflects Eros, the son of the Greek goddess of love and beauty, Aphrodite. Eros was named Cupid by the Romans, and it is his job to shoot the arrows of love, which was considered a form of madness, at surprised young adults. Eros was often depicted blindfolded to show that love is blind. But Eros has another role—to guide us toward our true destiny, which is to say, "Do what you love and everything else will follow naturally."

Upright

This is a card of cooperation, of working together with others to accomplish joint purposes. It stands for attraction of any kind, not only the romantic variety, and for any venture requiring harmony, union, and cooperation. A choice between two factors of equal worth may be required, but the choice you make will be the right one. Two or more forces or people may have come together in your life in pursuit of a common goal. This may be a temporary conjunction for some specific purpose, or it might be a long-term relationship.

Reversed

Your own disparate parts are cooperating with each other, and warring factors of your personality are coming together. You might realize you can be beautiful and brainy at the same time, or strong and gentle simultaneously. Whatever the case, you are resolving conflict and melding differences into a system of mutual support for yourself. Sometimes this card indicates a delay of some project that needs mutual cooperation or that you are trying to force cooperation among basically incompatible elements.

THE CHARIOT

THE CHARIOT is usually depicted as a strong figure holding the reins of two sphinxlike beasts, one black and one white. Sometimes the beasts are unicorns or other mythical creatures. The charioteer is fully armored and carries a scepter, suggesting royalty or that he is in the service of royalty. In some decks he wears a belt and a skirt decorated with zodiacal glyphs, symbolic of time. On his shoulders are crescent moons, indicating emotional factors and unconscious habit patterns that need to be changed.

In some decks the charioteer holds no reins—he uses sheer willpower to keep his steeds moving forward. The beasts pulling the chariot signify opposing forces, while the chariot driver represents mastery of these forces and control over inner conflicts. This card suggests that before taking on outer enemies or obstacles, it is essential to stop fighting yourself. The Chariot is a symbol for the self and its direction, as is any vehicle, such as a car, that appears in a dream.

❊ Interpretation

When The Chariot appears, there is a need to control competing forces, whether these are inner conflicts, people, or a situation in your life. Perhaps the solution to the problem at hand is to take the middle road between the conflicting elements. Once you have resolved the conflict within your own mind, you will be able to move forward. To do this, you need firm resolve—self-mastery. With clear thinking and a sense of purpose, you can overcome all obstacles.

The Chariot in a reading is generally favorable. It indicates you have the means to triumph over all obstacles and achieve the goals you have set for yourself. It can also mean that assistance is on the way. It may suggest you are in the process of transforming yourself and your ways of thinking and behaving to create a firm foundation from which to pursue your desires. You know how to use your past experiences to reach a goal, and you are in touch with deep inner resources to do so.

At a literal level, The Chariot relates to travel and transportation, so it can mean buying a new car or taking a trip.

The Chariot is related to myths in many cultures. Helios, the Greek sun god, drove a chariot of fire across the heavens. In the Hindu culture, Lord Surya drives his chariot along the road of time. In ancient Rome, the god of war, Mars, was depicted triumphantly riding to victory in his chariot. These mythic images suggest that the charioteer has triumphed over all conflicting forces, found his true path in life, and is now being guided by intuition and a clear sense of purpose.

Upright

Victory is assured! Things are moving fast. In this situation you are completely, totally involved, and happily so. Whatever task is at hand can be accomplished. Though the pace is faster than usual, you are attuned to the rhythm of it and the changes that are happening—at your job, in a relationship, or in some community or worldly situation. By uniting the yin and yang sides of your personality, you keep things going in the right direction.

Reversed

When The Chariot is reversed, the changes and transitions are happening internally, though still at a rapid rate. In fact, things are moving so fast that you may feel out of control and struggle to keep your head above water. It may seem that you are being pulled in two directions at once and are stressed out by the pressure. Choose a direction carefully and accept the process of inner transition as a positive one, but be clear about your direction in life. The more you can tune in to your own transition process, the more control over it you can exert.

STRENGTH

There is some discrepancy in how various decks number the **STRENGTH** card. The Rider-Waite-Smith deck shows Strength as number eight; other decks, however, show Justice as eight and Strength as eleven. This book follows Waite's ordering of the cards.

Many decks depict Strength as a woman alongside a lion. Some tarot readers see this as a struggle, but often there does not appear to be any conflict. In fact, she seems to be controlling the lion and may even appear affectionate toward him. Because the woman—or man in some decks—is unarmed, it's clear that she's using her inner strength to deal with the lion.

The woman may bend over the lion in a gesture of gentleness, closing his jaws as if she expects no resistance to her touch. Otherwise, she may be depicted caressing the lion, riding atop him, or standing beside him.

Although many interpreters view this card as emblematic of the struggle with one's animal nature, others see it as symbolic of self-confidence and inner strength. Though the lion is clearly the more physically powerful of the two, the woman represents human courage and willpower that masters the instinctive realm not by force but by cooperation.

✸ Interpretation

When Strength appears in a reading, you are exhibiting moral courage and fortitude. You have learned to work with your own instinctive nature, to listen to it and hear its whisperings. As in tales of the hero's journey, the seeker often meets with animals, representative of the instinctive realm, who guide and help him on his way. You have come through difficulties and learned to rely on inner strength to solve your problems.

This is a time when faith in yourself will pay off. You have made yourself strong by experiencing life's trials and tribulations. It is a time to let people around you know who you are—especially anyone who has been dominating you.

The indication is that stereotypically feminine traits do the work of reconciling our rational side with our intuitive one. In traditional mindsets, the feminine is always in closer touch with nature than the masculine. Females conquer animal natures not by brute force, but by gentleness and feeling their way into rapport with the instinctive side.

Depending on the placement of the card in the spread and the question being asked, Strength indicates that spiritual strength must replace or overcome physical strength.

TAROT TIP

Strength relates to the pagan goddess known as the Lady of the Beasts, who possessed understanding of the ways of nature. In ancient times, this goddess reigned supreme. Later, she was personified by the Romans as Diana, goddess of the hunt.

Upright

You have come through severe trials and triumphed. You have found your deep inner strength, and it will see you through whatever comes your way. You are firmly connected to the instinctual world (represented by the lion), and you are now able to make friends with it and control it. Your positive connection to your animal self will protect and care for you. Your inner drives are in harmony with your outer needs, and your instinctive nature supports all that you do or hope to do. At this time, your intuition should lead the way, not logical analysis.

Reversed

You are struggling to maintain your sense of self as you figure out what to do in a difficult and potentially harmful situation. As a result, your inner, instinctive nature is calling you to pay attention to your own needs instead of doing what others tell you. It is a time of hardship, but you will eventually overcome the difficulties and come out on top. Others may think you are behaving foolishly and not following the standards set by society. Regardless, your basic instincts of survival say this is a time for expressing your individuality.

THE HERMIT

THE HERMIT is a guide figure usually represented as an old man, often bearded, holding a lighted lantern aloft in one hand and a staff in the other. He may be dressed in the long robes of an anchorite or monk, plain and unadorned except for, in some decks, a knotted or tasseled cord around the waist. He radiates the wisdom of the archetypal elder figure.

The Hermit is generally shown standing, sometimes walking, looking ahead at what only he can see—your future. This ancient one now functions as a teacher and guide. Mountains in the distance suggest he has reached the heights and returned to earth to assist us in our development. He is wise in the ways of all the worlds, visible and invisible, material and spiritual.

The Hermit is linked to Father Time, or Saturn—the planet that symbolizes boundaries and limitations and the obstacles and lessons that appear on everyone's life course. His solitude suggests the periodic need to withdraw from the everyday world to regain perspective through self-care and reflection.

❋ Interpretation

When The Hermit appears in a reading, it can mean that a guide figure is at hand, offering help. You must make an effort to connect with this guide or consciously begin a search for the truth. A second interpretation is that the questioner must voluntarily withdraw from contact with the outer world to do some soul-searching. The universe cannot speak to you if you are distracted by the noise of everyday life.

The time has come to connect with your inner source, whether for guidance or inner balance. Sometimes the guide figure may represent a person, such as a counselor of some sort—perhaps a therapist—but usually it refers to inner guidance, or getting in touch with a guide from the other side.

The Hermit is linked to Uranus and Cronos, the god of time. The myth of these two fathers—both deposed by their sons because they refused to face up to the facts of their inevitable ends—warns us to accept the reality that all must grow old and die for new life to emerge. The death may not be a physical one, but rather the shedding of self-limiting ideas that hold us back.

✦ Upright

The Hermit waits patiently for you to turn to him for advice. You may be aware of his influence, but are ignoring it. You might actually be looking for guidance by isolating yourself in some way, seeking solitude, wisdom, and inner peace. You want to gain perspective on your life, and you are open to the inner guidance that is available to you.

✦ Reversed

Keeping busy can be a form of denial. You have been putting off giving yourself the solitude you need to sort out your life and the issues you are confronting. It is time—or long past time—for you to engage in self-reflection, to revisit your aims and goals, associations, relationships, career, and life path. You may want to withdraw to think things through; stop avoiding it.

THE WHEEL of FORTUNE

THE WHEEL OF FORTUNE card shows a wheel—often with eight spokes, a reference to the eight pagan holidays that mark the ever-turning cycles of life, death, and rebirth. The Wheel is also a symbol for the sun's path across the sky. Human or mythical figures may also be attached to the wheel, signifying that everyone is tied to the wheel of karma.

Some decks show a sphinx holding a sword at the top of the wheel, calmly watching as the wheel revolves. Occasionally the letters *Rota* are included in the card, a reference to the "Royal Road of the Tarot." There may be a jackal-headed man, called Hermanubis, who is known for keen eyesight, and a serpent descending the wheel, representing sexual or kundalini energy. At the four corners of the card many decks place winged creatures holding open books. These correspond to the bull, the lion, the eagle, and the man, symbols of the fixed signs of the zodiac, Taurus, Leo, Scorpio, and Aquarius, respectively.

Other decks show monkey-like figures or people in flowing robes caught on the wheel. Some depict eight young women between the spokes wearing expressions that range from joy to despair. The suggestion is that we are rising and falling through the various life cycles as the wheel turns. Occasionally, the wheel stands alone, perhaps decorated with symbols and suspended in the sky. Sometimes a blindfolded woman is turning the wheel.

✵ Interpretation

When The Wheel of Fortune appears in a reading, it means that something has been put in motion over which you now have little or no control. You must accept the action of the forces of destiny and align yourself with their aims. Generally, however, the outcome is considered favorable.

Changing circumstances, usually for the better, will promote your growth and advancement. The Wheel of Fortune is a reminder that every period of intense activity must be followed by a restful time of inactivity. Where you are in your own personal cycle will be shown by the other cards in the spread. This card almost always heralds good fortune coming as a result of what you yourself have put into motion, whether or not you're aware of what you have done to initiate the process. You may have applied for a new job, met a new person, begun a romance, decided to take a college course, or had a chance encounter that got the ball rolling—or the wheel turning. It means a new phase, possibly the need to make an important decision, or even a totally unexpected circumstance developing that will change your life.

Upright

You have done something—quit a job, made travel reservations, begun or ended a relationship, or opted out of a friendship or other situation. Destiny has been set in motion, and all will turn out as it is intended. There's very little more you have to do except to go with the flow. There may be unexpected turns of events, but they, too, are part of the grand plan for your life. This card is the precursor of good fortune.

TAROT TIP

The Wheel of Fortune is linked to the three Fates. One spins the thread of life, the second weaves it, and the third cuts it. Thus, The Wheel of Fortune is a reminder of the mysterious cycles of life, death, and rebirth, and of the invisible forces that measure them out to each of us.

Reversed

You are holding back your own destiny by refusing to make the necessary changes or take the required actions. This is causing stagnation and frustration. You think you are waiting for the right time, but fear of the unknown is blocking you. You may be fantasizing about what you want to do, but you have to take action before anything can happen. You may experience delays because of lack of commitment. Ask the universe to show you the way and fearlessly follow the direction you are given. Quit being wishy-washy and get on with what you already know you need to do.

JUSTICE

The **JUSTICE** card usually depicts a female figure, robed, sometimes armored and crowned. She holds an upright sword in one hand and in the other, perfectly balanced scales.

Unlike the contemporary image of justice as blindfolded, this Justice is open-eyed, suggesting that divine justice rather than human laws is at work here.

Interpretation

When the Justice card appears in a reading, it can indicate a literal interpretation that an actual legal matter is pending or being considered. Whatever the situation, you must weigh many factors to make a reasoned assessment, or judgment, of the matter. The Justice card urges you to seek guidance from your inner self, not to rely solely on human advisors. Also, it reminds you to think mindfully before taking action.

If other people are involved, consider their points of view, for issues of fairness are paramount now. Legal matters, if a part of the circumstances, should proceed smoothly, fairly, and in a dispassionate manner. Depending on what other cards appear in the spread, a third party could come to your aid and help you get the fair outcome you deserve. This card can also represent anyone involved with the legal profession: a lawyer, a judge, witnesses, or law enforcement officers.

TAROT TIP

Justice may describe a matter in which some sort of rectification is necessary, where wrongs must be righted, in a spiritual or personal sense, regardless of whether any laws have been broken. This is a card of karma and suggests you are reaping what you have sown. The card may be advising you to become more balanced or fair-minded.

Justice is related to the Egyptian goddess Maat, whose name means "truth and justice." She held a pair of scales upon which she weighed the newly dead person's soul against the Feather of Truth to decide if the soul was worthy to pass into the realm of Osiris, god of the underworld.

Upright

You are concerned with external circumstances, waiting for the right time to act. You may be seeking justice in personal or business affairs, or you may be involved with a lawsuit. In any case, it is important to resolve the situation in a way that is fair to all participants. You must create a balance, not only of power but in terms of your emotional reactions to the situation. This is a time for moderation in all things, for creating harmony to facilitate relationships. You may be called upon to arbitrate for others, or you may be subject to arbitration yourself. Your judgment is good at this time, and you are not swayed by personal considerations or bias.

Reversed

Justice in reverse indicates delays in legal matters or unfairness in a situation. If you are the person in power, you may be unduly severe in meting out punishment. If you are in the powerless position, you may be festering with resentment over being treated unfairly. Your equilibrium is out of whack, and you may swing from one extreme to another. The antidote is to balance your own life and become less dependent upon outside influences.

THE HANGED MAN

THE HANGED MAN is a tantalizing figure. Usually a male, hanging upside down by one leg, The Hanged Man's expression is serene, as if he enjoys his state. He almost appears to be engaged in a rather bizarre form of meditation or ritual.

In some decks The Hanged Man hangs from a tree. Its roots are in the ground and the crosspiece that supports him sprouts leaves. Some authorities say this is the Tree of Life itself. Around The Hanged Man's head there may be a golden halo, like the rays of the sun. Other decks picture only the horizontal beam, but it, too, sprouts leaves, showing that it is living wood.

❧ Interpretation

Many writers see The Hanged Man as a card of self-sacrifice and martyrdom, but others view this tantalizing card as voluntary surrender to the process of achieving enlightenment. It may require giving up superficial pleasures and trivial activities in pursuit of a more spiritual way of life. The word *sacrifice* derives from the Latin *sacra fice*, which means "to make sacred." Therefore, The Hanged Man may represent a sacred pursuit.

When this card appears in a reading, the person usually feels called to follow a less materialistic way of life. You are ready for whatever personal sacrifice is needed. You may need to pause momentarily and suspend ordinary activities to more clearly see your spiritual path.

TAROT TIP

Often The Hanged Man signifies going through a major transformation, perhaps caused by illness or some loss. The result has shaken up your old way of life and made you realize that there is more to life than money, material goods, and physical reality.

This card can indicate a need to develop the inner self. You might need to reevaluate what is and what is not important to you. It may be difficult to let go of old patterns—a relationship, a job, a worldview, a lifestyle—but letting go is essential to your continued growth.

The Hanged Man is related to all of the dying and resurrected gods of mythology. The Norse god Odin voluntarily hung for nine days from the tree called Yggdrasil, another form of the World Tree, to achieve knowledge of the runes and magic. In the pagan world, corn gods were sacrificed annually so that their blood, sprinkled on the fields, would produce an abundant harvest. In the Christian tradition, Jesus' crucifixion depicts this sacrifice.

Upright

You are suspended between the past and the future; a new direction for your life is in the making. Look at things from a different perspective and make necessary adjustments. The good news is there's no hurry: take your time and make the right decisions about where you truly want to take your life. Pay attention to your inner voice and be prepared to dance to a different drummer if need be.

Reversed

You are at a crossroads, but also at a standstill because you're stuck on the material plane and neglecting your spiritual development. Denying your real needs could be causing depression, dissatisfaction, or apathy. You feel that any effort will be futile. This is because you are not being true to your inner self. You may be sacrificing yourself because of a martyr complex or indecision. It's time to end such behavior and commit yourself to a worthwhile goal that will lead to your higher good, even if it means turning your world upside down.

DEATH

The **DEATH** card tends to frighten people, but despite its grim depiction, it symbolizes transformative powers. Many decks picture a skeleton with a scythe, wearing a black hooded robe. The figure may carry a banner on which is embroidered the mystical white rose, the symbol of pure and true love. The rose with five petals represents the five senses of material life combined with the immortality of the heart or soul.

A sun may be shown rising in the background, a sign of resurrection. Other decks show barren backgrounds; sometimes severed body parts lie about randomly. One deck features the decaying bones of a bird.

TAROT TIP

Death is related to the Hindu goddess Kali, who wears a necklace of skulls, and to the Greek Hades, god of the underworld, renamed Pluto by the Romans. Death corresponds to the number thirteen, which is the number of lunar months in a year.

☀ Interpretation

The Death card in a reading rarely foreshadows a physical death. Rather it means the end, or death, of a cycle. Whenever a stage in life ends, there is a need for mourning. Trying desperately to hold on to what is clearly over causes trouble. For example, continually getting cosmetic surgery to prevent yourself from looking older doesn't stop you from actually aging. The ultimate message of the Death card is the promise that new life follows disintegration.

Upright

Contrary to the grim illustration, the Death card indicates a transformation for the better. It does not portend actual physical death. Usually the person is experiencing a metamorphosis of some sort. Patterns you once found workable are no longer effective. The old ways must be destroyed to make room for the new that is coming into being.

✳ Reversed

You are putting off making necessary changes, usually out of fear. You feel that others are standing in your way, but you're really blocking yourself. You're stuck in old habit patterns that you know need to be changed, but you don't want to put forth the effort to alter them even though you are unhappy with the current situation. You may be depressed or in a state of apathy, the result of refusing to accept the necessary process of psychological death, which leads to rebirth. The way out is to face up to your stagnation, frustration, and unhappiness. Jettison any relationships that aren't working. Throw out the old and ring in the new.

TEMPERANCE

The lovely **TEMPERANCE** card often features a winged angel. The angel is usually depicted standing in a stream bordered by flowers, with the rising sun shining in the background. In many decks the figure pours liquid—the elixir of life—from a golden vessel into a silver one in a continuous stream, suggesting the interplay of the material and spiritual worlds and the eternal flow of the waters of life. Both the angelic figure and the cups are symbolic references to the traditionally feminine principles of cooperation, balance, harmony, receptivity, and creativity.

❊ Interpretation

Temperance, as its name suggests, is about moderation in all things. When Temperance appears in a reading, you are being cautioned to have patience, which can be a challenge for many people. However, the circumstances of your situation will teach you to wait calmly when it seems like nothing is happening.

The person who receives Temperance in a reading is not in a position to hurry matters along. The only course is to sit and wait for things to develop in their own time. The trick is to make the waiting constructive. Learning to do nothing mindfully is a milestone on the spiritual path—there are times when nothing can be done and nothing needs to be done.

Temperance is linked to the moon. Its number is fourteen, and on the fourteenth day after the new moon, the moon is at the exact midway point of its monthly cycle.

TAROT TIP

The word *temperance* is derived from the Latin *temperare*, which means "to moderate, blend, or mix together harmoniously." Interestingly, this card used to be named Time, which is a key to its underlying meaning.

Upright

You are being asked to blend things in a harmonious way. You are learning to temper your ego needs with the legitimate needs of the spirit within. This is a time of inner growth and outer harmony. With patience, you can unite the disparate elements—whether they are raw materials, resources, personnel, or ideas—into a harmonious whole.

Reversed

Things seem to be stalled. There's not much you can do at the present except to let things work themselves out, which they will in time. Patience is the key, for trying to force matters will cause bad feelings and poor results. This is a time to concentrate on blending the different parts of yourself—psychological, emotional, and spiritual—into a new form. Temper extremes that throw you out of balance.

THE DEVIL

THE DEVIL is often portrayed as a medieval Christian-type devil, complete with horns, hooves, a hairy tail, and a pitchfork. Usually at The Devil's feet are two small, humanlike figures, one male and one female, with chains around their necks. However, it is important to note that the chains are loose and the people could easily slip them off, suggesting self-imposed limitations.

The Devil is usually pretty scary looking. The Gilded Tarot portrays him as a muscular young man whose face is half-hidden beneath a helmet mask. In some decks he has an inverted pentagram over his head or on his brow.

The variety of illustrations implies widely differing opinions of the card's meaning. Some designers view The Devil as a creature of consummate evil; for others he is a mythical creature. Some people see The Devil as a symbol of human indulgence, ignorance, egotism, greed, and irresponsibility. Some decks go as far as to rename the card Oppression or Materialism to remove any religious connotation and focus on the material world.

❧ Interpretation

Superficially, The Devil appears to be one of the more alarming cards of the Major Arcana. However, he does not represent satanic forces with evil intent. He is the Horned God of pagan times, connected to the fertility rites banned by the Church, which feared the power of pagan rituals, especially those involving sexual activity.

When The Devil shows up in a reading, he is telling you to reevaluate your relationship to material things, which are keeping you chained. It's time to look at whatever is limiting your personal growth, especially abusive, obsessive, or harmful relationships. You may need to confront your fears about financial security and social and material success.

You need to recognize and acknowledge things you don't like about yourself—your personality, body, behavior, or temperament. It's time to let go of old fears, hang-ups, inhibitions, and ways you manipulate others to satisfy your needs instead of taking responsibility for yourself.

Often there is a sexual component involved that may have a harmful effect on your whole life. Or there could be a nonsexual relationship that binds you and that must end before you can grow further.

Whatever the situation, you are the only one who can change it. The two chained figures on the card represent bondage to the material realm. Their loose chains indicate you can attain freedom by relinquishing attachment to the things of this world.

◆ TAROT TIP

The Devil is related to the old pagan god Pan, a god of nature and the natural processes of the physical world, including sex. The Greek form of Pan was Dionysus, who cavorted with nature spirits and in whose honor uninhibited rituals that included a sexual free-for-all were held annually.

✳ Upright

The Devil represents the bondage that we create and maintain for ourselves. There may be obstacles in the environment that you find frustrating, or you may feel your options are narrowing. Someone else may be involved, but you have the ability to free yourself from the situation by using your willpower.

✳ Reversed

You feel trapped in a situation over which you feel you have no control, but close examination will reveal that your own attitudes and beliefs are causing the problem. Examine your beliefs to learn how they are restricting you. Be careful of any quick fix to your problems, which are actually structural and not superficial. If you are willing to do the hard work, both on the inner and outer planes, you can begin to live your best life.

THE TOWER

THE TOWER usually depicts a stone tower of fortress-like construction, such as those still remaining from medieval times. The Tower is in the process of falling down or being destroyed, often by fire or lightning.

In some decks The Tower's crown is being blown off by the fiery impact. The blast catapults human figures out of the windows. The implication is that the forces of heaven are angry and attacking the structure, causing flaming debris to fly out in all directions.

❖ Interpretation

Like the Death card and The Devil, The Tower tends to alarm anyone in whose reading it appears. But The Tower does not necessarily represent ruin and devastation, although its appearance usually does herald swift and dramatic change—sometimes extremely upsetting change.

You might have brought the situation on yourself by ignoring or denying that something needs restructuring or deconstructing. Most likely, you are already well aware of a pressing need to make changes, but haven't been able to take action. Then along comes a crisis, such as losing a job, getting a divorce, an accident, or a financial setback, and you have no choice but to face reality.

This card depicts the crumbling of an old, outworn structure, which you can liken to your life. It's time to deal seriously with your life collapsing all around you instead of, like the Roman emperor Nero, fiddling while your house burns. You might have to end an unsatisfactory relationship, quit a stifling job, cast off false values, shuck social conventions that limit your progress, or conserve money and live more simply. You can probably see how you are imprisoned by a self-created fortress, whether for protection, safety, or from fear of facing the unknown.

Destroy the old structures before they destroy you, so you can become free. In the wake of the chaos, a new order will grow. You can pick and choose among the rubble to decide what is worth saving, and from that, rebuild your life in accordance with who you truly are.

Upright

Whatever disruption or adversity The Tower is forecasting is for the best. The Tower represents overthrowing false beliefs and habits that don't serve you. In this sense, it is not a negative card but a positive one. There may be some kind of loss—personal or financial—but the catastrophic event could have been foreseen if you had been aware and willing to face facts. What is destroyed in conjunction with this card has served its purpose and needs to go.

Reversed

You are refusing to change old habit patterns, and you will suffer continued disruption in the form of unforeseen difficulties until you finally make some changes in your life. You may be confused about just who and what you are. At a deep level you are being prepared for the changes that must eventually take place, but you are resisting what your inner self knows already. Once you alter fixed beliefs and limited ideas you'll enjoy a new sense of freedom.

THE STAR

THE STAR usually portrays a nude female figure in or beside a pool of water, pouring from two jugs, one held in each hand. In many decks she kneels and pours the contents of one pitcher into the stream and the contents of the other into the ground, showing the connection between the two feminine elements: Earth and Water. The naked woman represents unveiled truth and purity. The jugs she holds contain the waters of life. Some of the water is being returned to the Source; some is being used to infuse the land with new life.

The background of this card displays stars. Many decks show seven subsidiary stars, sometimes arranged to reflect a portal, sometimes set in a circle or halo around the woman. The stars sparkle above a pastoral landscape. The colors are usually bright, often with yellow (the color of optimism) and blue (symbolizing peace) predominating, although some decks depict a nighttime scene.

✸ Interpretation

The Star is a universal symbol of hope. Its appearance can signal the end of the struggles represented by some of the earlier cards, symbolizing that a new and happier phase of life is coming. The shooting stars are harbingers of good luck.

A gate has opened for you to new possibilities. This card portends good fortune, creative inspiration, spiritual growth, help from unseen forces, and wishes come true. It marks a time of fulfillment.

The Star is linked to all the great goddesses of love and beauty from many cultures. Stella Maris, "Star of the Sea," was one of the titles bestowed upon the Roman goddess Venus. It is Venus who appears to us as the morning and evening star.

TAROT TIP

The Star corresponds to the number seventeen, which in old numerological systems was connected with immortality, hope, intuition, and self-expression.

Upright

At this time you are experiencing optimism and self-confidence. You feel good about yourself and your place in the universe. You have been preparing for this positive place. You are receiving assistance both from the invisible world as well as the material world. Good things are about to be manifested for you—money, possessions, love, recognition, or assistance—because you are flowing with the energy of the universe. You trust life's processes and are setting new goals for the future. New opportunities in your career or relationships are opening.

Reversed

When The Star is reversed, you are seeking your own path in a private way, without regard for the outside world. You may feel alone, withdrawn, or even resentful of outer obligations at this time. You may recently have experienced some disappointment that has caused you to turn inward. This is a necessary step. You need "repair time," including meditation and solitary self-care to realign yourself with your inner needs and reenergize yourself.

THE MOON is a magical, mysterious card emblematic of the unconscious and the invisible realm of dreams, imagination, and intentions. Usually the moon occupies the top half of the card, sometimes shown in both its full and crescent phases. In many decks, drops of water fall from the moon, raining down on two canines, usually a dog and a wolf, who bay at the moon. Some say these animals represent our opposite tendencies—the wolf, the untamed inner animal nature; and the dog, the domesticated, daily persona we show to the world.

There may be two towers, one on either side, symbolic of a portal. At the bottom of the card there is usually a pond from which crawls a crab (symbol of the astrological sign Cancer, which is ruled by the moon), or crawfish, or lobster. The water suggests the moon's link with the tides, the earth, the emotions, and the unconscious realm.

Interpretation

The Moon represents the link between spirit (sun) and matter (earth). The Moon symbolizes what we feel and how we respond. Emblematic of all that is instinctive and irrational, the moon affects everything and everyone on earth, from the ocean's tides to the moods and reproductive cycles of humans.

TAROT TIP

The Moon card can point to a need to nurture yourself or to care for your health. For artistic people, its presence in a reading may mark a time of increased imagination and creativity.

When The Moon appears in a reading, it suggests that you should pay more attention to your inner self, your lunar self. In the moon's diffuse light, you can often see more clearly than in the glare of the noonday sun. The light of the sun enables you to see the world around you, but the moon illuminates what springs naturally from inside you. Pay attention to your dreams, feelings, instincts, and intuition.

The Moon can also indicate deceit, self-deception, confinement, and undoing, but these conditions are usually a result of ignoring your own inner promptings. If you get "taken"—especially emotionally—it's because you let your rational mind override your feelings. The Moon's appearance also recommends tying up loose ends connected to the past, especially to your mother or other females.

The Moon is the symbol for the Goddess, whose three aspects are depicted in the moon's phases. As the newborn crescent, the moon is the maiden, the virgin—not chaste, but belonging to herself alone, not bound to any man. At the full moon, she is the mature woman, sexual and maternal, giver of life. At the end of her cycle, the waning moon represents the crone, whose years have ripened into wisdom.

Upright

The Moon says that you are becoming more aware of feelings and inner perceptions. The Moon also suggests psychic ability. You can tune in to other people's vibrations because you are connected to the energetic network around you. Pay attention to hunches and dreams. This is also a good time to develop your intuitive skills.

Reversed

Your soul is calling for help, trying to get your attention. You may have been ignoring your lunar needs—self-nurturance, artistic expression, and receptivity. The demands of the day—the masculine side—are overwhelming you, and you need time out to reconnect with your feminine side. You have allowed the pressures of the outside world to throw you out of balance, and you feel disconnected from your true self. It's time to rest and reflect.

THE SUN

THE SUN card features a blazing sun, sometimes with a face. Beneath the sun, a popular image is of a smiling nude child riding a white horse.

Some decks show two children with their arms around each other; other decks picture a young couple holding hands. The child or children are clearly very happy. The astrological sun rules children, creativity, pleasure, and the heart. The Sun card represents life itself, for the sun gives life to everything on earth. The Sun suggests vitality, confidence, achievement, and success in all endeavors. The Moon symbolizes the Goddess and feminine principle, whereas The Sun represents the masculine principle.

✷ Interpretation

Your past work is now bearing fruit, a concept that is symbolized by the child or children on the card. Whether the fruit represented is an actual child or a creative project, the outcome is a happy one. Good things now come into your life: success, achievement, health, good fortune, and happiness.

When The Sun turns up, it brightens any negative cards in the spread. Its influence is always beneficial, suggesting prosperity, enthusiasm, honors, public recognition, and achieving your goals. You are happy to be alive because you feel it is the dawning of a new day. Efforts or ventures will turn out favorably.

✷ Upright

Generally considered a positive card, The Sun indicates vitality, confidence, success, and good times. It signifies a time of new beginnings, of things going well, of accomplishment, success, and contentment. You feel cheerful and self-confident, full of life and energy, ready to undertake new projects with enthusiasm. You may be starting more than one project, or upgrading something in your life, such as taking a more satisfying job, remodeling your home, or moving to a sunnier climate.

✺ Reversed

All of the upright information still applies to the reversed Sun, because it is never a negative card. However, the reversed position indicates that there will be delays or that you will have to make some adjustments you hadn't planned on. You might have to exert more effort to produce positive results. Now is the time to explore new and more effective ways to express who you are to the outside world.

◆ TAROT TIP

The appearance of The Sun in a reading can foreshadow a reward for your previous striving and suffering with "a day at the beach." The Sun card might indicate you are going to take a wonderful vacation in the sun, where you can relax and let go of your worries.

JUDGMENT

The **JUDGMENT** card visually seems rather negative. In many decks, a winged figure, whom some call the angel Gabriel, emerges from a cloud and blows a trumpet. There may be several nude figures looking up, hearing the trumpet's blast. Of all the allegorical symbolism of the Major Arcana, this is the most purely Christian, suggesting the feared Day of Judgment, when God will judge all souls and apportion out rewards or punishments accordingly. However, this is not a totally Christian idea; the Egyptian goddess Maat, for instance, weighs the soul against her Feather of Truth.

Whatever the viewpoint or deck design, the symbols on this card suggest an awakening.

✵ Interpretation

When the Judgment card appears, it suggests that you are having a personal awakening. Sometimes the card coincides with turning away from a traditional set of beliefs toward one that better suits your personal philosophy of life. Judgment represents the end of an old way of life, a cycle that is finished. It is a time to seek a new direction, to make adjustments that reflect who you truly are.

Generally speaking, this is a positive card symbolizing regeneration and rebirth after a period of confusion and confinement. You may have felt "dead" in your old life. When Judgment appears, you have the unique opportunity to enliven yourself and your environment by making the appropriate changes. It's a time of freedom to be yourself.

TAROT TIP

Judgment relates to the Greek god Hermes, called Mercury by the Romans. The deeper expression of Hermes-Mercury's role as messenger of the gods is a figure who mediates, or delivers messages, between the conscious mind and the unconscious realm.

❧ Upright

You've had a wake-up call from the universe and are now ready to step into a new phase of your maturing process. Your life is fairly settled now, and you are letting things grow at a steady pace, without hurrying the process. A new phase in your life is coming into being as the natural result of your maturity—like a tree that has gone through the flowering stage bears fruit as the product of its maturity. You may get important news that will prove beneficial, or you may learn something new that will bring you joy and a sense of fulfillment. Your health improves, and problems are easily solved.

❧ Reversed

Interior factors are at work, but you have little or no control over them. You may be thinking about making some changes. Emotionally, you may be called upon to grow up. Even if you aren't sure just how to handle what's happening, you must make peace with the changes. Judgment reversed can also indicate frustrating delays or postponements, possible loss or separation, and the need to cope with life changes.

THE WORLD

In many decks **THE WORLD** card shows a young woman, either nude or wearing a long scarf. In each hand, she holds a double-ended wand that points both upward and downward, suggesting "As above, so below."

The four corners of the card usually feature a bull, a lion, an eagle, and a man—representing the four fixed signs of the zodiac: Taurus, Leo, Scorpio, and Aquarius. These elemental figures also depict the four directions.

Interpretation

This is the last card of the Major Arcana. It represents balance and support by unseen forces and symbolizes the end of the spiritual journey begun with The Fool. To embark upon the spiritual journey is to invite unseen forces to interact with us. These creative energies manifest in many ways, and often serve as guides. You are entering a place of great powers and, sometimes, great secrets. As you interface with this world, your life will undoubtedly change. Here you connect with supreme power—not the power of the material world but of the invisible order that supports and nourishes our world and our lives.

When The World card appears in a reading, it is a signal that you have been guided to the successful conclusion of your spiritual journey. At this, the final stage, you will receive what is rightfully yours because you have earned it. You feel whole, complete, refreshed from your long journey and ready to begin anew at a higher level.

Upright

Success in all endeavors is assured. Everything is available to you, and all is right with the world. Whatever you do now will prosper—a career change, a move to another place, a new relationship, recognition, rewards, acclaim. This is the end of an old cycle and the beginning of a new one. You have mastered the complexities of your inner nature and feel supported by your inner resources. This is a time of supreme self-confidence and victory. You have put your trust where it belongs—in a higher power—and you will reap the rewards. Many possibilities and opportunities are available to you, and you are free to choose what pleases you.

Reversed

You are being presented with a multiplicity of choices and aren't sure which one to make. You may be experiencing new facets of yourself. Or you may be rejecting new ideas being offered out of fear or a limited understanding. Now is the time to face the fact that the universe is a more complex place than you have been willing to admit. Your goals are in sight, but they may be more complicated to achieve and require persistent and determined effort on your part.

INTERPRETING THE MINOR ARCANA

 INTRODUCTION TO THE SUITS

The Minor Arcana include the court cards (typically called King, Queen, Knight, and Page) along with numbered cards (Ace through Ten) for each of the four suits (Wands, Pentacles, Swords, and Cups).

These suits help us pinpoint the areas of life that need our attention, because each of the suits represents a distinct realm of activity, experience, and personal growth. When many cards of the same suit appear in a reading, it's a clear indication that the person consulting tarot is concerned about a particular area of life—or should be. A reading about a relationship will usually turn up several cards in the suit of Cups, whereas Pentacles are likely to predominate in a reading about finances.

What the Suit of Wands Means

The Wands are linked with creativity, drive, energy, enthusiasm, willpower, and outer world activities. They describe attitudes, abilities, and situations that offer the potential for success, perhaps through your talents and imagination. Artists and craftspeople, for instance, may find that Wands appear in their readings frequently. This is the suit of entrepreneurs who may not be making big bucks but are doing what they have always loved.

Generally speaking, Wands are positive cards. The colors tend to be bright (yellow stands for optimism, red for action), and the designs or scenarios depicted are usually cheerful. Wands may be symbolized as branches sprouting leaves or flowers, wooden staffs, crude clubs, poles, scepter-like rods, or flaming torches. As representative of the Fire element and masculine force, Wands are obvious phallic symbols.

KING of WANDS

The **KING OF WANDS** is usually shown as a dignified man, seated on a throne, robed and crowned. Sometimes he wears armor; other times he appears as a prosperous merchant king. A positive and powerful figure, he is clearly in command of the situation, confident and at ease. He holds a full-length staff or rod, generally upright but sometimes leaning against his shoulder. In some decks this King faces sideways, and whether he is looking toward or away from other cards in a spread will have a bearing on his relationship to the reading.

Upright

Upright, the King represents a man of status and wealth, an influential and independent person who helps those he cares about. He may be a boss, mentor, senior business partner, or advisor. You can rely on his honesty, intelligence, loyalty, and fair-mindedness, and you are sure to get good advice from him. If the King does not represent an actual person in your life, the card can refer to a situation, which is exactly as it appears to be, with no hint of deception. This card can indicate that good fortune is coming your way, perhaps in the form of unexpected help or advice, good news, a promotion, or an inheritance.

Reversed

The King of Wands reversed indicates delays in a business or creative project; however, nothing really problematic is standing in your way. If the King represents a person, he won't block your efforts, but he won't go out of his way to help you either. He may approve of what you are trying to accomplish on your own and lend moral support…but don't expect overt or tangible assistance.

QUEEN of WANDS

The **QUEEN OF WANDS** is pictured as a statuesque woman of regal bearing. She holds a tall staff in one hand, a symbol of her authority. Often she sits on a throne, robed and crowned, but some decks show her as a well-dressed matron figure.

Upright

Socially prominent, this Queen represents a woman who is in a position of authority and shines in her endeavors. A "lioness"—warm, generous, and loving—she is honorable, creative, intelligent, friendly, and mature. Her advice is well worth taking, and she will be a loyal confidante or provide valuable assistance. A natural leader, she may be the head of a business, social, or philanthropic organization, or a political figure. If this Queen does not represent an actual person, the card indicates that now is a good time for you to move forward in a business or creative venture. If the Queen represents you, you have the qualities within yourself that you need to succeed.

Reversed

If the Queen of Wands is reversed, she can represent a powerful woman who demands control over your affairs in return for her advice, support, and/or financial assistance. She wants to control social situations for her own advantage. If the Queen does not represent an actual person, the reversed card can be a warning to be careful in any business deals with women. She also advises you to avoid offending socially powerful people, and to be aware of deception, greed, and jealousy.

KNIGHT of WANDS

The **KNIGHT OF WANDS** is usually depicted as a young man on a rearing horse, moving forward. He brandishes a wand-like weapon, but it seems more for show than to render a blow. He usually wears a suit of armor that is colorful and ornate. His position indicates that he is riding toward some encounter, more likely a joust than a fight.

Upright

Knights are messengers and travelers, and the Knight of Wands brings good news concerning work or social activities. His glad tidings may relate to almost any anticipated happy event—a journey or vacation, a change of residence or job, an engagement or marriage. If this card represents a specific person, it refers to a young man who is a relative or friend with the same qualities as the King and Queen, who are his parents in the royal family. The person bearing the message can be trusted and is faithful.

Reversed

Even when reversed, the Wands aren't particularly negative, but the reversed Knight can indicate a delay in a message or paperwork you have been expecting. A trip may be canceled because of bad weather or an engagement or wedding postponed, even broken off. The reversed Knight can represent separation from people, places, or situations.

PAGE of WANDS

The **PAGE OF WANDS** shows a young person, generally facing sideways and holding a tall staff before him with both hands, perhaps leaning on it. His attitude is expectant but casual. He wears clothes similar to those of the rest of the royal court, but because he is young, he may wear shorts. Some contemporary decks depict the Page as a girl or an androgynous figure.

Upright

The Page of Wands represents an important positive message regarding your current project or situation. It usually references work, although it may be of a social nature. If the card represents a person in your life, it could be a younger relative or friend, an apprentice, student, or assistant. This Page is an enthusiastic adventurer and may be interested in international travel, foreign cultures and people, the arts, or philosophic projects.

Reversed

When reversed, the Page of Wands represents a delay, which could cause trouble. Something you were expecting might not arrive on time, or a mix-up may occur. Or the Page may bring a message of unwelcome news that causes some disruption in your life or requires you to travel to put things right. If this Page represents a person, he is untrustworthy or conveys false or misleading information. Be on guard.

ACE of WANDS

The **ACE OF WANDS** is usually pictured as a large wand, sometimes with shoots sprouting out of it. Some decks picture only a wand, often one that is large and elaborate, like a ruler's scepter or a magician's ceremonial tool.

Upright

This Ace indicates the beginning of an enterprise, usually involving business, the arts, or finance. It shows that you have planted the seeds for a new birth—possibly a creative or moneymaking idea. You are now free from restraints that have hampered you in the past, able to express yourself successfully, take on a new role, or forge a new identity through your work.

Reversed

The Ace of Wands reversed indicates that the process of creating a new identity or the start of a new endeavor has not yet manifested. It's still in the planning stages. You may experience delays, or you might have to rethink your plans and make adjustments. You know you have the potential to do something new, but you might hesitate because of lack of resources or confidence.

TWO of WANDS

The **TWO OF WANDS** is an ambiguous card. It shows that a second, perhaps unexpected, factor is entering into the situation at hand. There is an element of surprise. Sometimes this card indicates a choice must be made, which could be related to your work or a creative endeavor.

Upright

You are saying yes to a new enterprise with the expectation that you will achieve ownership, wealth, and good fortune. You've started something and are awaiting results. You may, however, have to deal with some unforeseen problems or encounter unexpected obstacles and opposition, such as a bank loan not coming through, a partner taking off, or a loss of support you were counting on. Sometimes this card can indicate a need to alter your course.

Reversed

This position suggests you may be in for a surprise, perhaps a nasty one. Whether the surprise element portends good or bad will be indicated by the surrounding cards in the reading. If the Two of Wands appears with a court card, for example, it may mean the person the court card represents will disappoint you or make an unexpected appearance, changing the situation.

THREE of WANDS

The **THREE OF WANDS** represents someone who is ready and willing to demonstrate what he has achieved. You can remain calm and in control of the situation, for there is no need for impulsiveness. This is a time to take things firmly in hand and to act in a mature and responsible manner based on your experience and common sense.

Upright

You have consolidated your situation, business, or enterprise and now can expect financial and/or personal gain. By clearly defining the role you want to play, you present a positive picture to the world. This confident attitude may draw helpful people toward you or attract beneficial circumstances. You've established a solid foundation for your business or occupation and can expect cooperation from others. At this point, you are clear about who you are and what you intend to achieve. Others will respond positively to you.

Reversed

You are doing most of the work on an internal level, clarifying your needs and planning your sense of direction. You have resolved most of the problems connected to the situation or enterprise and negotiated the tricky parts. Now you can expect things to go smoothly when you do go public with your ideas.

FOUR of WANDS

The **FOUR OF WANDS** is an extremely positive card, indicating that your efforts to establish a project, business, or other endeavor are successful. Your position is secure and comfortable. Now you can relax and enjoy life. It's a time of respite and rejoicing.

Upright

You are enjoying pleasure and prosperity, reaping the rewards you have earned. Your finances are in good shape, and you are in harmony with your environment and the people in it. You've shown the world who you truly are and what you can achieve. It's a time for celebration and good times.

Reversed

The reversed position of this positive card means you are celebrating your good fortune in a quiet way. You may be expanding your property holdings or creative output without fanfare. Financial gains may be more modest than if the card were upright, but you are satisfied with your accomplishments and the sense of having done a job well. Your public image, your relationships, and your sense of self are favorable.

FIVE of WANDS

The **FIVE OF WANDS** is about competition in economic, social, or career areas. It signifies the mad scramble for money and power, success and recognition, with the accompanying excesses of greed and corruption. This card represents struggle in the marketplace. It can also indicate that you are involved in ego-based battles with other people in your workplace or the social arena. Often the image on the card shows five men fighting among themselves, using their wands as weapons.

Upright

New factors moving into the situation demand that you change, adapt, and grow. Life's not as simple as it was. New competition has moved into the neighborhood—or the industry—and you have to put forth more effort to keep what you have gained. Depending on the rest of the reading and how you handle the challenges facing you, you could either suffer hardship and loss or go on to greater success and prosperity.

Reversed

When the Five of Wands is reversed, you must change and adapt to different and difficult circumstances. The new competition may be cutthroat, dishonest, or underhanded. There could be litigation to resolve disputes, and your public image may suffer. Don't get involved in questionable or risky practices at this time and be careful whom you trust.

SIX of WANDS

The **SIX OF WANDS** represents triumphing over adversity. A card of victory, it indicates good news and success. You've met the challenges to your position, work, or reputation and come through with flying colors.

Upright

Victory is at hand. You have overcome or conquered the opposition. Past self-doubt has been resolved, and you are in the process of winning some significant battles. You can expect to succeed and have your desires manifested. Gifts may be received; awards and recognition won.

Reversed

The hopes and wishes you have for your success are being delayed, often by factors over which you have no control. You feel frustrated and angry, ready to do battle to get things set right. You're being challenged by circumstances to take a stance about who you are and what you intend to accomplish. You may have experienced some kind of betrayal that has caused you to reevaluate your self-image.

SEVEN of WANDS

The **SEVEN OF WANDS** is about courage and determination. It indicates you are willing to fight for what you believe in and will stand your ground. Previously, you might have fallen into complacency, but now you are ready to face challenges.

Upright

Profit and gain come only after you have firmly held off your competition or enemies. You may be outnumbered, but your determination will win the day. You are discovering inner resources you didn't even realize you had and using them to overcome obstacles. Thus you have the advantage and will eventually achieve success by sheer force of will and motivation.

Reversed

This position signifies a time of confusion. You don't know whether to hold on or back off, but now is the time for firmness and decision. Even if you're not sure which way to go, it's one of those situations where any decision is better than none at all.

EIGHT of WANDS

The **EIGHT OF WANDS** is a card of movement, action, and excitement. Things happen rapidly, and success is assured. Follow through on what you've already put in motion and start planning new goals.

Upright

You have shot your arrows into the air, and they are speeding toward the target. Now is a time for initiating the next phase of your enterprise. This may involve air travel or other movement. It's an exciting and hopeful period when you are likely to be extremely busy. Positive things are rapidly unfolding. Establish the roles you want to play and let go of those that no longer suit you.

Reversed

Movement may be unwanted, stressful, or unpleasant, such as being transferred across the country when you'd rather stay put. Go with the flow, wherever it leads. Allow yourself to be open to new experiences, but be prepared—be aware of what you're getting into. Relationships—marriage, business partnerships, family—may suffer. You might be required to reprioritize your schedule to accommodate other people's needs.

NINE of WANDS

The **NINE OF WANDS** represents defending your legitimate territory. Through effort and determination, you have protected what's yours, shown courage under fire, and stood your ground. This is a card of recovery. Now you are in a strong position, and success is at hand.

Upright

Nines represent completion, and the Nine of Wands in a reading indicates that the job is done. You have had the discipline and the ability to plan well and wisely. Your relationships are developing positively, and you are moving forward with a sense of purpose and direction. If there is still opposition, your skills, strength, and courage will prevail over all opponents.

Reversed

You may be fighting a losing battle. If so, it's time to cut your losses and get out. Whatever it is, it is over, and if it hasn't worked out for you, then move on to something else. Learn whatever lessons you can from the failure and know that the wheel is always turning.

TEN of WANDS

The **TEN OF WANDS** shows you taking up new responsibilities appropriate to the new cycle that's beginning now. These may seem burdensome, but you have the strength and character to shoulder them. You feel you can do anything at this time, even an extremely difficult task.

Upright

Your labor may have gone for naught, or you may be carrying burdens that really don't belong to you. You feel weary, as if the whole world is on your shoulders. It's up to you to decide whether to continue carrying the heavy responsibilities you have undertaken or if other people are shirking their part and should help out. Sometimes one member of a family or organization gets all the dirty work for the simple reason that they are willing to do it. Make sure others are doing their fair share. Ask for help if you need it; don't let pride stand in your way.

Reversed

The burden is lifted—sometimes unexpectedly—and there is a feeling of freedom from undue responsibilities. Either you have taken the appropriate action or are about to do so. In any case, your load has been shifted, reproportioned, or removed entirely. You are learning to delegate and take on less. Pressure and stress are reduced, and you are able to enjoy life more. Sometimes, however, depending on negative influences in the spread, you may be suffering the consequences of overload—either with ill health or burnout. You may need a recovery period.

What the Suit of Pentacles Means

Pentacles are often depicted as discs of gold, sometimes with a star (pentagram) or a five-sided design (pentagon) in the center. Interestingly, the pentacle is a powerful symbol in magick, used for protection against harmful influences, so there is also a suggestion that money and material resources can provide protection.

The suit of Pentacles (or Coins) has come to represent people who deal in the economy: financial professionals, accountants, entrepreneurs, real estate agents, or retailers. It includes bankers, lawyers, businesspeople, stockbrokers—in other words, many of today's middle- and upper-middle classes. Pentacles can also symbolize those who desire to upgrade themselves financially, who understand money and how it works, and who respect the power it confers. In a reading, Pentacles usually point to an increase in finances, and can show success in business, a raise, or relief from financial difficulties.

Therefore, in general the appearance of Pentacles is a positive note. As Pentacles represent the element Earth, they also indicate groundedness in the material and physical world. They can suggest concern about financial security, career, or whatever work you do as your livelihood. In some instances, Pentacles describe other types of material resources, physical capabilities, or health conditions.

KING of PENTACLES

The **KING OF PENTACLES** is usually shown as a royal figure regally dressed and seated on a throne. He may or may not be crowned, but he appears comfortable with the power money confers. Generally, the King holds a single coin in one hand and a scepter in the other, and he is sometimes depicted as a prosperous merchant.

Upright

This King represents a mature man who is not only wealthy but also courageous. A solid citizen, he is reputable, dependable, and kind to others. He symbolizes worldly power in a positive sense and is experienced in handling money matters. He is cultured and refined and can provide reliable counsel on matters of money, property, and security.

If the King represents an actual person, that person is likely to be in an important position in your life—possibly he is a leader where you work, your boss or backer, or a banker from whom you are soliciting a loan. If the King is not an actual person, then the appearance of the card indicates that you are engaged in some worldly enterprise that will meet with success.

Reversed

Some people consider this King reversed to be a negative symbol, representing danger or an unwise business move. Others view the card as a warning to be aware of the small print in any contracts being negotiated. The King can also indicate unfair competition, shady business practices, or an untrustworthy man.

QUEEN of PENTACLES

The **QUEEN OF PENTACLES** is a benevolent figure with a regal and kindly bearing, sometimes shown holding the pentacle or coin in her lap and gazing fondly down at it. She may also be pictured standing, leaning against an ornate throne or chair. She is someone who understands and respects money as a tool but does not worship it.

Upright

This Queen represents a generous woman who is also an excellent manager in practical and financial areas. She may be a sensual woman who is at home in her body and enjoys her creature comforts. As an advisor, she will be fair. She is pragmatic and realistic and wants to see that the money she distributes produces tangible results. If the card doesn't represent a person, it shows a harvest after much labor, security, and smart use of resources.

Reversed

In the reversed position, this Queen may represent someone who will try to block your efforts. She could be merely indifferent or actively hostile. If she is a relative or an older friend, mentor, or boss, she might be a superficial person who only pretends to want to help you. Or the price of her help might be too high; she wants to control everything. She may lack confidence and try to compensate for her own shortcomings by a display of her wealth, or she may be hiding a lack of money. If this card does not represent a person, it describes a situation where you should be cautious about whom you trust.

KNIGHT of PENTACLES

The **KNIGHT OF PENTACLES** usually brings good news concerning money. He is typcally depicted on horseback, facing sideways, wearing armor, and holding the pentacle before him as if offering it to someone. Unlike the Knight of Wands (who is on a charging horse), this Knight's horse is at parade rest, calm and stable. He is poised on the edge of adventure or travel.

Upright

If this Knight represents a person, he's someone with the spirit of adventure, but who is practical and materially minded. He is good at performing any task set for him, but is not likely to be a self-starter. If the card does not signify a person, it suggests a situation involving arrivals and/or departures. You may quit a job for a more lucrative one elsewhere, move to another locale for financial or work-related reasons, or experience other changes in your life relative to money, possessions, or security.

Reversed

The Knight reversed brings an unwelcome message about money, often a loss of some kind, a disappointment, or frustration due to an unforeseen delay. Existing plans may have to be aborted; delays could cause failure. If the card represents a person, he may be a young man who is unemployed or uninterested in employment. If it's not a person, this Knight shows a situation where waste, inertia, and problems with money exist.

PAGE of PENTACLES

The **PAGE OF PENTACLES** is often shown as a young person standing in a countryside. He holds the pentacle before him, as if admiring it. His attitude suggests that he wants money or at least the means to gain it, perhaps through education. Sometimes called the card of the student or scholar, the Page of Pentacles shows one who is so intent on his lessons that he misses everything else going on around him. In some contemporary decks, the Page is pictured as a girl or androgynous figure.

Upright

The Page of Pentacles indicates good news regarding the acquisition of money or material goods. His appearance suggests someone who is intelligent, refined, sensitive to the arts, and appreciative of the good life. Ambitious and determined, he is goal oriented. If he does not represent a person, this card indicates your own worldly ambitions and/or a message concerning them.

Reversed

This Page in the reversed position reflects someone who is lazy, unmotivated, or uninterested in furthering himself through education or work. If the card does not represent a person, it may indicate bad news concerning money matters. It can also refer to some sort of disappointment, such as failing an exam, not getting into the college of your choice, or not being hired for a job. More effort and focus are needed.

ACE of PENTACLES

The **ACE OF PENTACLES** often depicts a large pentacle as the central image on the card. Some decks illustrate the coin in a decorative manner, like a shield. The Ace of Pentacles is the card of new financial opportunities or successes, new money, new enterprise, resources, ambition, opportunity, and acquiring material goods. In some cases, it can also represent physical or health-related benefits.

Upright

This Ace is extremely positive, predicting success for some new enterprise you are starting. You are planting the seeds for a new venture involving the acquisition of money or financial security. The Ace is a strong indication of prosperity coming to you. Be open to receive the benefits it promises.

Reversed

This Ace in the reversed position indicates that your new venture is still in the idea stage. You are laying the groundwork to achieve a greater level of security and prosperity. Your material gain will come, but it is being delayed, and you must be patient and persistent. Don't get discouraged.

TWO of PENTACLES

The **TWO OF PENTACLES** suggests either money coming from two sources or having to juggle finances to make ends meet. In some cases, it shows a financial or business partnership. It is a positive card indicating good fortune and enjoyment. You may be experiencing financial difficulty, but it won't last. Better times lie ahead.

Upright

A message about money could be on its way to you. You are still in the stage of deciding which of two different options to choose. Perhaps you are worried about money, or taking a side gig to make extra money. It's time to make a choice and stick with it even if you aren't sure of the outcome.

Reversed

You may be experiencing financial difficulties while pretending that all is well. You are juggling not only sources of income but also options for change—but this isn't the right time to make a change. Hang in there until the right moment presents itself. You need to overcome doubt and have faith in yourself.

THREE of PENTACLES

The **THREE OF PENTACLES** is the card of the craftsperson, someone who has already developed skill in a profession or trade. It's time to turn these skills to profit, and success is assured. The Three of Pentacles usually shows you are planning and conferring about a future action, such as cooperating in a business venture.

❀ Upright

You are acquiring marketable skills, preparing yourself for action in the world. Perhaps you're a recent graduate or have gone back to school to upgrade your skills or change your career. You are enterprising and may be interested in a career in business or finance. You can anticipate a rise in prestige and earnings. This card can also indicate a payback period when you demonstrate your abilities and begin to reap the rewards of your efforts. Or you could receive money that's owed to you.

❀ Reversed

You aren't making the effort to acquire the new skills you need in today's changing marketplace. You may be stuck in a job you really don't like but lack the confidence or ambition to strike out and change things for the better. Get going—thought without action is useless.

FOUR of PENTACLES

The **FOUR OF PENTACLES** indicates a security-conscious person who is holding tight to money and material possessions. You may fear that loss is in the offing and are trying to prepare yourself by closely guarding what you have. Or you may simply be overly cautious and conservative in financial areas.

Upright

You are hanging on to something—either your possessions or a situation—in a stubborn and inflexible manner. Fear of change may be involved, or you may merely be comfortable where you are. Your fixed attitude, however, may be limiting you and blocking new opportunities for success and happiness.

Reversed

You may be trying to make something happen prematurely, or you are holding on too tightly to your current circumstances. Perhaps you are quarreling with someone over money, such as in a divorce proceeding. You need to loosen up and have more trust in the universe to provide solutions.

FIVE of PENTACLES

The **FIVE OF PENTACLES** is the only Pentacles with a fundamentally negative connotation. It suggests financial losses, business problems, or material lack. It can also indicate that spiritual bankruptcy is at the root of this unfavorable condition. In some instances, this card can show that your priorities should be spiritual, not financial or worldly.

Upright

This Five is a warning that money may soon be very tight, that losses may ensue from ill-advised investments, or that support you had counted on won't be forthcoming, such as a grant, estate of a loved one, or bonus. In some cases, it advises you to ask for help—from other people or the universe.

Reversed

You are being advised to get your house in order financially. Cut your losses any way you can to avoid further deterioration of your finances; if you are in debt, focus on getting it paid off as best you can. Be extremely careful of any future investments. Don't take risks at this time.

SIX of PENTACLES

The **SIX OF PENTACLES** shows that past financial problems have been resolved. Your income is steady and your security is stable. You are in a balanced position concerning income and outflow. You are using your prosperity to help others. Because Sixes represent give and take, this card can also indicate a business partnership or shared financial responsibility.

Upright

Good things are coming to you and going out from you, in material terms. You are experiencing abundance, prosperity, and personal fulfillment. You may be in a position to support a good cause, perhaps by contributing financially or volunteering your time or expertise. This card can also represent philanthropic projects or providing work for other people.

Reversed

You need to recoup after a period of loss and confusion. You want to help others, but you don't have the means, and that makes you unhappy. You may be required to find a lifestyle that will create a sense of security for you so that you can find peace of mind.

SEVEN of PENTACLES

The **SEVEN OF PENTACLES** indicates receiving the benefits that you have earned by your own hard work. Like a farmer harvesting crops that he has nurtured through bad weather, you are reaping what you've sown. The harvest may still be a ways off, however, so keep tending your fields.

Upright

You've put in the time and effort and paid your dues. Now you will gain in your business or other enterprise. Not only that, but you feel great satisfaction from a job well done. Growth and good fortune are yours, well earned.

Reversed

You are experiencing disappointment or failure in some enterprise. Financial difficulties, usually the result of unwise monetary decisions, may be causing you concern. It's a time to take responsibility for how you use money.

EIGHT of PENTACLES

The **EIGHT OF PENTACLES** is a card of craftsmanship and conscientious work. It suggests developing and applying your skills in a productive manner. You know what you want and how to go about achieving it—so if you are sincere and persevere, your efforts will succeed. A business or project will prosper as a result of refining your craft or improving your processes. A new venture brings success because you are training yourself intensively with a clear goal in mind.

Upright

You are integrating old skills into a new form, or you are adding new skills. You've tried various means of making your living, and you are now finalizing how you want to use your personal resources to fulfill your needs and expand. Your sureness of purpose guarantees success. Your craftsmanship will be rewarded by increased income, opportunity, and respect.

Reversed

When this card is reversed, there is an indication that you have not mastered the necessary skills to achieve your goals. You may desire to begin some new enterprise, but a lack of ambition, ability, or clarity prevents your success. More effort or education may be necessary.

NINE of PENTACLES

The **NINE OF PENTACLES** suggests that you are free from financial concerns and worries. You are in a period of abundance thanks to your good decisions in business or financial affairs. This card says you've arrived, accomplished your goals, and now feel secure.

Upright

You have integrated the factors of your life into a secure base. Now you are enjoying money, resources, and physical energy as a smooth combined flow. There is plenty all around you—material well-being, order, safety, and success.

Reversed

Your security is shaky, and you may be dependent on someone else—perhaps a spouse or relative—for your financial well-being. Circumstances may have caused you to lose your independence. Figure out how to regain what you've lost.

TEN of PENTACLES

The **TEN OF PENTACLES** is a happy card, indicating a solid and secure life, both in business and with your family. Your work and planning have paid off, and you are enjoying the fruits of your labor.

Upright

You are emphasizing home and family at this point, now that you have a secure income to support them. You may be planning to buy a car or that house you have always wanted. Family matters are at the forefront, and you have the leisure to concentrate on personal affairs. This card can represent a time of financial security such as marrying into money or receiving an inheritance.

Reversed

You may be so established at this point that you are stagnating. Maybe you have retired comfortably but are just sitting around watching TV. You need to activate some growth in your life to avoid boredom. Take up a hobby, do charity work, or teach others your skills.

What the Suit of Swords Means

The Swords symbolize events, conditions, situations, or attitudes that may be difficult or challenging. However, as a result, they also represent the growth and development of the conscious mind. When Swords appear in a reading, you may be experiencing stress or problems, but these are making you think.

The suffering associated with the Swords can also be the result of overanalyzing situations. In our modern society, where left-brain logic is favored over right-brain intuition and feeling, Swords can represent the alienation that comes from cutting yourself off from your inner self.

The Swords are often depicted as unsheathed double-bladed sabers, sometimes as daggers or the witch's tool known as an athame. Although usually shown as battle swords, they suggest power and authority wielded for some purpose other than physical fighting. Some writers interpret the Swords as totally negative, others see a spiritual side to the Swords as well as the obstacles, pain, and difficulties sometimes associated with them. This is because we sometimes come to a spiritual path through suffering of some kind, be it physical, mental, psychological, or emotional.

KING of SWORDS

The **KING OF SWORDS** is a somewhat stern figure who is in absolute command, but who can be trusted to be fair in his judgment and decisions. He is usually pictured enthroned, armored, helmeted, and crowned, a combination of symbols that suggests not only power and authority, but also a willingness to use them forcefully if necessary. Sometimes he holds a set of balanced scales suggesting both justice and the sign of Libra. The suit of Swords corresponds to the element of Air; therefore, his appearance often has to do with your mental processes.

Upright

This King represents a man of great strength and authority. If he stands for a person, he is involved with mental work, such as a researcher, a lawyer, a teacher, someone in the communications field, or a military officer. As such, he is a good counselor with acute mental dexterity. He has a gift for thinking clearly and rapidly, and he is able to express his thoughts with considerable eloquence. If this King is not a person, he represents a situation in which mental and communication skills are called for. When he appears, you may be on the verge of a spiritual breakthrough and are ready to communicate it to others in your life.

Reversed

When reversed, this King indicates fickleness; using words as swords to wound; gossiping; superficiality; playing one person against the other; or rigidity of opinions. If he does not signify a person, he can represent a situation in which the people around you are hostile toward your ideas or your spiritual quest. You may have to keep these matters to yourself.

QUEEN of SWORDS

The **QUEEN OF SWORDS** is the female counterpart of the King, except that she represents the intuitive and creative side of the mental processes. A mature woman who sits on an ornate throne and wears beautiful robes, she holds her sword in one hand and reaches out with the other in a gesture suggesting permission to rise and come forward. She is a formidable figure with power and authority, either in the mental or spiritual realm.

Upright

When the Queen of Swords appears in a reading, she may represent a single or independent woman with authority and power. Often she is someone with impressive intellectual or communicative abilities—a writer, professor, lawyer, minister, businesswoman, or scholar. If she describes a person, the Queen may be someone who has endured a painful loss, but she draws upon her willpower and experience to continue on her path. If she does not represent a person, this Queen can indicate that you are going through a difficult experience, which will open new opportunities for positive growth. This is especially true if an Ace appears in the reading too.

Reversed

When this Queen is reversed, it means you are not dealing well with a loss. There may be sadness, withdrawal, or mourning beyond reasonable expectations. If the card does not stand for a person, it can represent a situation in which you are bogged down emotionally, wallowing in pain.

KNIGHT of SWORDS

The **KNIGHT OF SWORDS** is often shown leaning forward on a charging horse, his sword held as if he is ready to encounter an enemy. He is definitely on the attack, and by his expression he expects to win the battle. He can represent a person who is overly aggressive or argumentative, who lives in attack mode. Or he can mean that you are aggressively pursuing a lifestyle that will allow you to live out your own philosophical ideals.

Upright

As a messenger, the Knight of Swords may bring bad news that relates to you personally or to someone close to you. Some kind of conflict is at hand, usually of a mental nature. There could be substantial differences of opinion around you, with angry messages being sent and received. If this Knight is not a person, you may be so focused on your intellectual pursuits that you are neglecting other facets of your life. You may be expressing your ideas too forcefully and antagonizing the opposition. Diplomacy may be called for.

Reversed

When reversed, this Knight loses his aggressiveness and becomes passive about a situation that requires action. He suggests you are delaying doing what is necessary, perhaps neglecting necessary grunt work or communication. Unfortunately, there could be serious repercussions from avoiding this work. If this card is not a person, it can indicate that you are mentally closed off from a situation that desperately needs attention, thereby creating bad feeling and opposition.

PAGE of SWORDS

The **PAGE OF SWORDS** indicates risk on a mental or spiritual level. It might mean you are taking up some new line of thought or study. Many decks depict a young person who seems a bit unsure of his ability to wield his weapon, although he tries to appear as if he can easily defeat any enemy. He usually wears a short tunic made of leather or padded cloth, instead of armor. Some contemporary decks show the Page as a girl or androgynous figure.

Upright

As a messenger, this Page brings news of problems and difficulties, perhaps relating to a younger person you know. Your child or younger sibling may have failed college exams or be in trouble with the law. An element of experimentation is indicated here—either you or someone else is taking a risk or behaving in a risky manner that might cause problems. The Page is motivated by unconventional activity that can cause strife. Overconfidence or the ignorance of youth might also get this person into trouble.

Reversed

The reversed Page is having trouble getting it together. Although this young person is attractive and charming—eager, confident, clever, active—he isn't strictly on the right track. This Page could represent someone who is sponging off others, maybe parents or friends. Or it could indicate someone who is bad-tempered or capable of spiteful action. Insecurity lies at the root of this person's actions.

ACE of SWORDS

The **ACE OF SWORDS** indicates a new beginning. Most decks depict an upright sword, sometimes crowned at the tip. The Sword and crown are decorated with living vegetation—vines, flowers, leaves, fruit. This Ace indicates a triumph over difficulties through the use of mental means or spiritual growth. It is emblematic of a major breakthrough.

Upright

A brand-new lifestyle is beginning. You have achieved this opportunity through willpower and by making smart decisions. Prosperity, recognition, new development—especially spiritual growth—are sure to follow in the wake of your new direction in life. This Ace signals a birth, usually of an idea or enterprise. You now are in a position to manifest your intentions in a new way.

Reversed

As this is an extremely positive card, the reversed position indicates only delays or glitches. What you planned for on the spiritual plane may not manifest on the physical plane as quickly as you had hoped, and this may be causing frustration and tension.

TWO of SWORDS

The **TWO OF SWORDS** represents a situation in which it appears impossible to move forward. Because you can't figure out with logic or intellect how to proceed, you must rely on blind faith that the universe will handle things.

Upright

This card indicates that you are stuck for some reason. You may be maintaining the situation by putting up a facade and ignoring the underlying tension that exists. This is an uncomfortable position to be in, but you aren't ready to do anything about it yet. You need to speak up and communicate clearly. Eventually, however, change must take place. You have choices. Remove the blindfold and look honestly at the situation.

Reversed

When the Two of Swords appears reversed, it exacerbates the severity of your situation. You feel helpless to make the necessary changes. One party may be unwilling to admit to the truth of the situation, making discourse impossible. This may result in deceit, disloyalty, or duplicity.

THREE of SWORDS

The **THREE OF SWORDS** is a card of severance, signifying separation and sadness, perhaps the end of a romantic relationship. However, there is the sense that the separation or breakup was needed. Although you feel post-breakup blues, the separation was meant to be. This card can also mean you feel isolated and cut off from something you love—a way of life, your home and family, a philosophy, a pursuit, or a job.

Upright

You are feeling the pain of separation, possibly a romantic one. Sometimes this card can signify a love triangle. A third party has entered into the formerly stable situation and caused the breakup, but it was ready to happen anyway. It's time to let go. Whatever relationship has died must be allowed to disintegrate spiritually too. Don't try to hold on to the past.

Reversed

You are taking this separation too hard and not accepting the truth of the situation. You may be blaming someone else instead of acknowledging that you were partly responsible for the breakup too. You may be suffering from depression, unable to move past this difficult situation. Don't get bogged down with what might have been, though. Seek professional help if necessary.

FOUR of SWORDS

The **FOUR OF SWORDS** is a card of respite after the sorrow or misfortune of the Three. It represents rest and recuperation, of working on your problems quietly and with motivation. You feel the need for introspection and solitude, to contemplate and understand what happened and why.

Upright

After a painful time you are in the first stage of recovery, whether from emotional upheaval or physical illness. You are resting and taking time to think things through and plan your next moves wisely. You may want to retreat from other people and the world while you get your inner house in order.

Reversed

You are not allowing yourself the rest and respite you need, and if you continue this way you could make yourself ill. You need a period of calm and quiet in the wake of a major disruption. Refusing to make time to recuperate, both physically and emotionally, will only worsen the situation.

FIVE of SWORDS

The **FIVE OF SWORDS** suggests the double-edged nature of the sword. One edge signifies defeat, misfortune, betrayal, and loss; the other suggests learning to accept the boundaries we all must face and live with. Fives are about adjustment, and this Five indicates you are adjusting to some kind of change brought on by distress or loss. It's an uncomfortable process but a necessary one.

Upright

Change is part of life, and the more you resist it, the more difficult you make things for yourself. Whether you need to change your exercise habits, your self-care routines, your self-limiting beliefs—now is the time to address those things that are holding you back.

Reversed

Your losses have hit you hard, and you are in a state of great unhappiness. You feel hurt and betrayed, angry and discouraged, but only you can pull yourself out of your misery. You may feel confused about why the crisis occurred, but deep down you know the reasons. You just don't want to face them.

SIX of SWORDS

The **SIX OF SWORDS** indicates that you are putting past troubles behind you. It marks the beginning of a new phase after a time of upheaval. You have rebalanced yourself and are enjoying a new peace of mind. This is the calm after the storm—a period of smooth sailing with relatively few problems ahead.

❋ Upright

This is a time of integration—or reintegration. Harmony and ease prevail. New people you can trust come into your life. After some intense suffering, you now feel optimistic and balanced. This card can also indicate a move or a journey over water. The destination may be unknown, or the effects of the move may be uncertain, but luck is on your side, and any change you make will go smoothly.

❋ Reversed

As this is a positive card, the reversed position simply means delays, or that the harmony you are experiencing is internal rather than being expressed externally. You may have come to a new way of thinking about your life, or you may be affirming your old beliefs and attitudes, finding a path that's comfortable for you.

SEVEN of SWORDS

When the **SEVEN OF SWORDS** shows up, it urges caution in all dealings. Secretive action or indirect communications may be occurring behind your back. Nothing is quite what it seems to be, and you have to use your wit to achieve your aims. Be wary of overconfidence. You may appear to be on top now, but being too cocky could do you in.

Upright

You have the upper hand over a tricky situation, but you still need to exercise caution. Discretion and discrimination are required, as are diplomacy and maybe even evasive tactics. You may not enjoy this oblique approach, but you'll be more likely to achieve success this way.

Reversed

When the Seven of Swords appears reversed, it emphasizes all of the upright messages but includes the possibility of deception. Maintain caution and vigilance in all things during this period. Stay open-minded and flexible so that you can respond to changes quickly. You may be experimenting with different plans of action, getting various points of view.

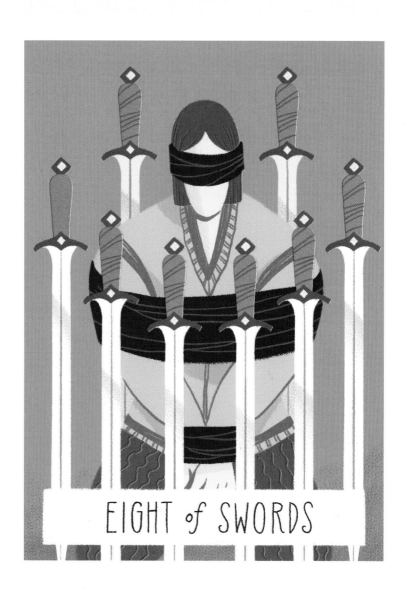

EIGHT of SWORDS

The tension of the **EIGHT OF SWORDS** is related to that of the Two, except that the Two indicates denial, while the Eight suggests you are conscious of the choices available. Despite this, you feel trapped—either unable or unwilling to choose and therefore stuck in a painful state. You are your own worst enemy.

Upright

Most writers view this as an extremely negative card. The card describes a situation that causes great unhappiness, but you can change matters. The bad situation is temporary, and, if the card falls in the "future" position, the problem can even be avoided.

Reversed

This card reversed warns that what is already wrong can get worse, or that a difficult situation is approaching. Make sure all your affairs are in the best possible order. If you've been putting off paying your taxes, getting insurance, or settling some legal matter, take care of it promptly. Your well-being depends on using your head and preparing for unexpected emergencies.

NINE of SWORDS

The **NINE OF SWORDS** shows extreme anxiety, nightmares, tension, unhappiness, and regrets over past mistakes or misfortunes. When it appears, you are in an unhappy and tense state of mind, whether or not the facts bear out the fear. Thus the suffering associated with this card may be mostly in your mind.

❈ Upright

The Nine of Swords indicates that you are troubled by bad dreams or horrible fantasies. Deep-rooted or repressed issues are trying to surface so you can resolve them. It will likely be very challenging to change your attitudes and beliefs, but it's worth the effort and unpleasantness. Nine is the number of completion; thus, this card indicates that the changes you are being required to make forecast a better future.

❈ Reversed

The Nine of Swords reversed shows intense mental anguish. It's time to examine belief systems that no longer apply to your life and that are standing in the way of your progress. You are suffering because you refuse to face the cause of your problems. Honesty is called for if you are to resolve the situation.

TEN of SWORDS

Although the **TEN OF SWORDS** is another difficult card, its appearance marks the beginning of the end of a period of trials and tribulations. It also signifies the start of a new cycle. But first you have to clear away the debris of the old cycle and often this process is painful. Stress and exhaustion may accompany the appearance of this card.

Upright

When the Ten of Swords appears upright, it suggests that you need to make a clean break from the past and its attendant pain and suffering. Whether this means a divorce, quitting a job, moving across the country, or changing a belief system, make the break cleanly, leaving no loose ends. Do away with previous illusions that have clouded your vision and try not to worry.

Reversed

When the Ten of Swords appears reversed, it indicates that you are holding back, reluctant to take the necessary steps to move into a new cycle. You are delaying actions or deceiving yourself about a situation. You may be making excuses for yourself or someone else to maintain the status quo, but you are only prolonging your agony. Make a choice, even if it's the wrong one.

What the Suit of Cups Means

The Cups describe emotions, love, romance, social relationships, culture, comfort, intuition, and the unconscious. The love shown by these cards is not just romantic love, but friendship and love of one's fellow humans as well. Kindness and compassion are depicted in the imagery of this suit. Thus the Cups are almost always considered positive. If there are negative factors in the reading, a Cup card will mitigate the bad omen, help to make a situation better, or point the way to a solution.

In most decks the Cups are pictured as large, beautiful, often ornate vessels or chalices. Sometimes they appear double-ended as if they could be filled from either side.

KING of CUPS

The **KING OF CUPS** has a loving demeanor. He is a mature man, usually pictured seated on a throne, often with water in the background. Rarely is he shown wearing armor—usually plain robes—so there is nothing of the militant about him. This King's expression is benign, his attitude relaxed and nonthreatening.

Upright

This King indicates a man who is kindly disposed—a benevolent father figure, who may represent your own father or someone who fills that role for you. He can also signify an older man with whom you either have or want a romantic relationship. Whether as a friend, advisor, or lover, he is utterly trustworthy and dependent, and he can be relied upon to come through for you when you need him. Most interpretations consider this King to be a man of culture, interested in the arts, possibly himself a creative type. If the King does not represent an actual person, the card indicates a situation that is favorable, especially in an artistic pursuit.

Reversed

Your involvement in a relationship involving love is ending, but the process should not cause much pain. It's time to move away from dependency on an older person—perhaps your father or a mentor or teacher—and strike out on your own. Whether the circumstances are related to a person or to your own inner psychic process, the result is the same. It is also possible that this King reversed represents someone who is trying to get rid of you for some reason, romantic or otherwise. You need to let go and, if necessary, mourn the passing of something that was good once but is now over.

QUEEN of CUPS

The **QUEEN OF CUPS** is a beautiful and benevolent figure. She holds an ornate chalice and gazes at it as if she could see visions of the future inside. She wears flowing robes, and her crown is elaborate but grace-ful. Usually she is pictured with water flowing at her feet, for this suit corresponds to the Water element. An affectionate and loving woman, whether wife, mother, friend, or lover, she is wise in the ways of the human heart. Her attitude is one of receptivity and approachability.

Upright

The Queen of Cups can represent any kindly woman in your life—a wife or the woman you love. She is creative, perhaps an artist, with visionary tendencies. Her psychic ability is highly developed and tends to be accurate. However, she tempers her intuitive nature with mature judgment. If she represents you, these qualities apply although they may still be undeveloped. If this Queen does not represent a person, the situation she describes may concern a creative endeavor, relation-ship, or circumstances with a positive emotional tone.

Reversed

This Queen reversed can indicate a love relationship gone sour, or someone who is having trouble expressing emotion. If the card rep-resents a person, it can be a dishonest advisor. Be careful whom you trust with your secrets and your emotional life. If the card represents you, it can mean that you are playing with possible dangerous psychic or emotional matters you don't understand.

KNIGHT of CUPS

The **KNIGHT OF CUPS** is usually portrayed as a handsome young man sitting upright on a white horse in parade or dressage position. He holds the Cup out in front of him. His helmet may be winged, a symbol of the messenger. In this case, he brings a message of love or good tidings. Usually depicted in an outdoor setting, sometimes with water under the horse's hooves, this Knight is armored only lightly. He's a lover, not a fighter.

Upright

The Knight of Cups is bringing you a message about love, or he may represent your true love—the knight on the white horse! His appearance indicates you are deeply involved in an emotional situation, to the point where little else matters. You may be awaiting this message—such as a declaration of love or a proposal of marriage—with such anticipation that everything else seems insignificant. If the Knight does not represent a lover, he is certainly a friend who is honest, intelligent, and willing to aid you.

Reversed

The message you hope for has been delayed or may never arrive. The relationship you yearn for may be based on deceit or superficiality on the other person's side. You may be obsessing about someone who really doesn't care that much about you and who will never make a commitment, even if he has led you to believe he is sincere. This person is fickle, likes to flirt, and isn't likely to settle down.

PAGE of CUPS

The **PAGE OF CUPS** usually shows a young man in decorative clothes wearing an elaborate hat. His attitude is relaxed and open, and he seems pleased with himself. Some decks depict the Page as a girl or androgynous figure.

Upright

This Page signifies a young person, male or female—possibly a son, a daughter, or a younger sibling—who is bringing you a message about love. It might mean an engagement or a wedding—or some situation that holds an inherent emotional risk. The circumstances may be exciting yet scary at the same time, as with a sudden elopement. Often the Page suggests naiveté or vulnerability, especially in matters of the heart. If the card represents you, it says you have already decided to take an emotional risk. You are willing to give it your all because you feel things will work out.

Reversed

The Page reversed shows a fishy situation, something you should look at carefully. If the card represents a person, deceit may be involved—flattery for gain or secrecy in matters of the heart. Someone may be trying to seduce you, and you are blinded to the falseness of his or her intentions. Or you may be playing the role of the seducer, toying with someone's emotions. If so, take care. You might get hurt yourself.

ACE of CUPS

The **ACE OF CUPS** shows a single large chalice, usually with water flowing fountain-like out of it. This Ace suggests a fountain of love or the Holy Grail. The Ace represents a gift, in this case a gift of love, either personal or spiritual.

Upright

The Ace of Cups indicates a new beginning—a new love or a one-on-one relationship of any kind. Previously unfelt emotions come into play now, perhaps as a result of seeing a relationship in a new way. This Ace can also herald a birth—of a child or an idea. This is a fertile time for emotional or creative growth, as this Ace symbolizes the consummation of something hoped for.

Reversed

When reversed, this Ace indicates delays or disappointments in love. Sometimes a new beginning doesn't develop as hoped. Difficulties in getting a new relationship or creative effort off the ground could be indicated, or something you are trying to set in motion meets unforeseen and frustrating obstacles. Perhaps this is not the right time to start something new.

TWO of CUPS

The **TWO OF CUPS** describes a coupling of some sort—a marriage, a partnership, a union. Harmony is in the air. You may be in the honeymoon stage of a relationship or endeavor when all seems right. This card can also represent a new stage of happiness and harmony in an existing relationship.

Upright

You are moving in tandem with another person now, and all is going smoothly. Whether it is a romantic relationship or a friendship, you feel accord, mutual admiration, and goodwill toward each other. Ordinarily, this card refers to a love match, but it can also indicate a partnership of another sort.

Reversed

This card has such a harmonious vibration that its reversed position isn't much different from the upright one. It can suggest delays, or that the relationship may have to be kept a secret for some reason.

THREE of CUPS

The **THREE OF CUPS** signifies that something has been brought to completion. It shows victory and success. The act of falling in love signified by the Two of Cups may have resulted in a baby, or a creative venture has produced a viable product. It's time for a celebration!

❋ Upright

You are experiencing success and plenty; a time of joy and celebration is at hand. Your feelings are clear now, and you understand your emotional patterns in a positive, growth-producing way. You're on your way to great things.

❋ Reversed

The Three of Cups reversed remains a positive influence, except that the gratification you are getting may be more sensual than deeply emotional. You will still enjoy success, but your achievements may be in small things.

FOUR of CUPS

The **FOUR OF CUPS** represents a state of apathy and withdrawal. However, this may be a necessary rest after the hectic excitement represented by the Three. It's a time to get away by yourself and just relax and recenter yourself for a while before getting back into your daily grind.

Upright

You are withdrawing your emotions from a situation or a person. After intense emotional involvement, you may need some space for yourself. There's a feeling of letdown after a buildup, as in the postpartum blues or when you have to deal with all the nitty-gritties of making a marriage work.

Reversed

You may be experiencing displeasure, disappointment, or dissatisfaction with a relationship or the way a creative project is turning out. You want to withdraw to regain perspective and balance.

FIVE of CUPS

The **FIVE OF CUPS** signifies that you are brooding over past wrongs, losses, disappointments, or hurts. You are dwelling on a painful past and refusing to look forward to a positive future.

Upright

Your unhappiness is a result of your attitude, which you can change. This is a card of choice. You can continue to ruminate over what went wrong, or you can contemplate how things can be better in the future. You don't have to be miserable.

Reversed

You are in a state of indecision. You are refusing to make up your mind about something or to face facts. Just because there have been past losses doesn't mean there can't be future gains. If you continue in this negative state of mind, you will only make things worse.

SIX of CUPS

The **SIX OF CUPS** signifies nostalgia and happy memories. This card refers to a sentimental remembrance of things past. These pleasant and comforting memories can be used to better your future, to build on. Knowing that you have been happy in the past will enhance your ability to be happy in the future.

Upright

You are experiencing emotions connected to your past that will shed light on your future. You are feeling calm and collected about past events, putting them into perspective, and beginning to understand how they can bring a bright future.

Reversed

The Six of Cups reversed suggests changes in the immediate environment that will make you feel more secure. These may involve meeting new friends or making new associations. You are developing new emotional tools that will aid you in the future. An important event is coming soon.

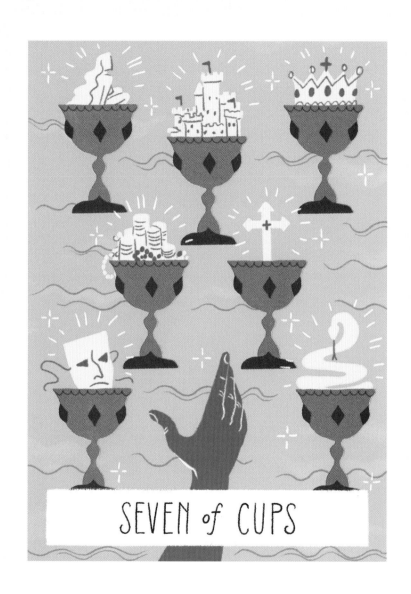

SEVEN of CUPS

The **SEVEN OF CUPS** signifies a time of great creative potential, along with the energy to make use of it. Many options are available: the difficulty is in choosing the right one. This card represents fantasy and imagination.

❋ Upright

You are looking at a number of possibilities now—too many to make an easy choice. With so many options, you are exploring different intentions in your imagination, but deciding which to manifest is a challenge.

❋ Reversed

You are confused because too much is going on. You need peace and quiet to sort through the multiple choices confronting you. Let your feelings be your guide.

EIGHT of CUPS

The **EIGHT OF CUPS** usually means that the only solution seems to be to turn your back on a situation and go in another direction. What's there isn't working as expected or isn't important anymore. You know what you want and won't settle for anything less.

Upright

You wish things were different, but they aren't so you have to let go. Cut your losses and get out of a situation or relationship that has failed despite your best efforts. Turn your sights and your energies toward something that is likely to be more fulfilling.

Reversed

You are running away without facing your problem. Things haven't worked out as you hoped, and you want to bolt without giving the situation a second chance. If you split now, you may regret it later.

NINE of CUPS

The **NINE OF CUPS** is the best pip card in the entire tarot deck. Sometimes called the "wish card," it indicates great joy and happiness, dreams coming true, and getting what you wish for. It's like winning the lottery and meeting Mr. or Ms. Right on the same day.

❧ Upright

This card means success, triumph, everything you want and hope for. When the Nine of Cups appears, make a wish. Ask yourself, "What do I really want?" The card responds: You will get it.

❧ Reversed

It's hard to say anything negative about this card, even in the reverse position. Relax, have faith in the universe, and don't get in your own way by trying to control things.

TEN of CUPS

The **TEN OF CUPS** represents contentment, real love, domestic bliss, and satisfaction in all your endeavors. It symbolizes people living harmoniously together, sharing their love and their lives unconditionally. This card is so favorable that it can offset any negative cards in a reading.

Upright

This card is an indication of everything that most people wish for—love and harmony, a happy family life, true love and companionship. It signifies a time of completion, of reaping what you have sown. It symbolizes abundance in a larger sense.

Reversed

Delays and obstacles block the happiness you long for. Circumstances beyond your control may be the cause, and at the moment there's nothing you can do but keep a positive attitude. Hold tight and wait for things to change, which they will.

Chapter

6

TAROT SPREADS

INTRODUCTION TO SPREADS

Every tarot card reading starts with a spread. A *spread* is just a fancy word for a "configuration or arrangement of cards"—usually three or more, and up to more than a dozen—designed to convey certain types of information. You could think of a spread as a puzzle that presents a picture when all the pieces are in place. Spreads are the tool that tarot readers use to ask questions of the cards and receive the answers.

This chapter contains different spreads—some simple, some complex. Choosing the right spread is sometimes the most important act in a reading. Don't be misled into thinking that the simple spreads aren't as informative—they can sometimes provide just the insight you need, whereas a larger spread may convolute the question and provide you too much detail.

In a spread, each position within the overall pattern means something specific. A question or topic is assigned to each location. The relationship between the cards also becomes as important as the individual cards themselves. It is wise to look at the how the artwork of each card flows into the scene from the cards that surround it. Is the Knight of Wands rushing toward The Devil card or away from it? Just by looking at how the cards interact with each other, you can start to answer your question before you even dive into the prescribed meanings of the cards.

You'll probably find that some spreads appeal to you more than others or are more useful for your purposes. Some readers and books

TAROT TIP

By combining the meanings of the cards with the meanings of the positions in a spread, the insights provided are increased exponentially.

will tell you that the Celtic Cross is a "must have" in your tarot spread arsenal, but there are plenty of professional tarot readers who never use that spread. No one spread is better than another; the choice of which spread(s) to use is yours entirely. After you become experienced at working with tarot, you might decide to design your own spreads or adapt traditional spreads to suit your life.

THE SIGNIFICATOR

Some individuals like to use a Significator, a card that symbolizes the person for whom the reading is being done, to start a reading. This card will "anchor" the energy of the reading to the person or the topic chosen. Usually this card is incorporated into the spread, although sometimes it is laid to the side, faceup, before a reading begins. In some cases, a Significator could represent a group, an organization, a situation, or an event.

Usually, a court card is used as a Significator for a specific person, however, a Major Arcana card can also be used if the individual's characteristics strongly correlate with the card. A man who is a titan of industry and CEO of a company may better be described with The Emperor card than the King of Pentacles. Use your intuition to decide which card is perfect for the individual or situation.

TAROT TIP

Many tarot readers do not use a Significator card. If it does not feel right to use one, just proceed with the reading without a Significator.

SHUFFLING THE CARDS

There are as many methods to shuffle a tarot deck as there are card readers. Some readers prefer a "riffle shuffle" which is the typical shuffle you use with playing cards, while others prefer the "hand over hand" method of moving the cards about. Other individuals may even prefer just to fan the cards in front of them and then pick from that stack. Find a method that works for you—don't think too hard or put too much stress on the process.

Here's an easy step-by-step guide to shuffling:

First, decide what type of shuffling feels best in your hands. Tarot cards are typically bigger than playing cards, so for some individuals, a riffle shuffle may be difficult.

Next, decide if you want to shuffle a certain number of times and then stop, or if you want to just stop when it "feels" right to stop shuffling.

Then decide where to choose a card from the deck—do you take the first card off the top or fan them out and choose from there?

Once you find a shuffling and card-choosing rhythm that works for you, try it out for a while before changing it.

When reading for other people, some readers like to involve the person in the shuffling process, either handing the deck for them to shuffle or allowing the client to "cut the deck" before selecting the cards. Whether or not to allow another person to touch and use your deck is a personal preference. Again, do what feels right for you and your situation.

The Single-Card Spread

This is the easiest and most basic of all spreads, and it can be used to answer all types of questions. Although you won't get as much information as you would from a longer, more complex spread, this method can be surprisingly helpful—especially in answering straightforward questions for which you need an immediate answer.

Shuffle and cut the cards while thinking about your question. Then draw a single card from the pack. You can either pick the top card from the deck or fan out all the cards facedown and select one at random. The card's meaning will shed light on your question.

Two Cards: The Either/Or Spread

Use this spread when you have two options and can't decide between them. After shuffling and cutting the deck, select two cards either from the top or at random from the pack. The first card represents one option; the second card signifies the other choice.

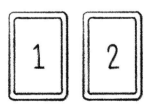

The Three-Card Spread: Representing the Past, Present, and Future

This three-card spread lets you see the past influences or conditions regarding a situation, the present state of the matter, and what's likely to occur in the future. After shuffling and cutting the deck, select three cards either from the top of the pack or at random. Lay them out side by side. The card on the left represents the past; the middle card shows the present; the card on the right indicates what's likely to occur in the future.

Overcome Obstacles: The Four-Card Spread

This spread offers advice for dealing with a specific concern. Its strength is its simple, direct approach to dealing with practical, every-day problems. Shuffle and cut the cards, then lay four cards out side by side in a horizontal line, from left to right, and examine them.

CARD 1 Situation   **CARD 3** Action recommended
CARD 2 Obstacle   **CARD 4** Outcome

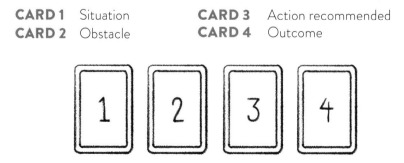

The Traditional Celtic Cross Spread

This popular and versatile spread calls for a Significator. Place it on the table to bring you (or the person for whom the reading is being done) into the reading, then lay Card 1 on top of the Significator. Continue laying out the rest of the cards in the following pattern:

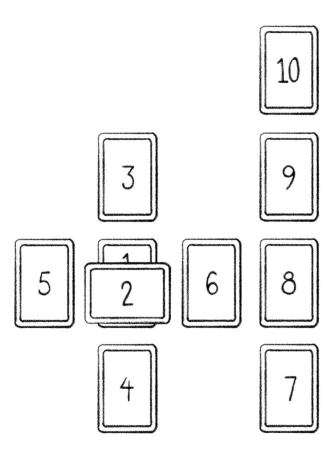

CARD 1	This covers you and describes your immediate concerns.
CARD 2	This crosses you and describes obstacles facing you.
CARD 3	This crowns you and describes what is known to you objectively.
CARD 4	This is beneath you and describes the foundation of the concern or past influences affecting the situation. It can also show what is unknown about the situation.
CARD 5	This is behind you and describes past influences now fading away.
CARD 6	This is before you and describes new circumstances coming into being—the near future.
CARD 7	This is your self and describes your current state of mind.
CARD 8	This is your house and describes the circumstances surrounding the situation.
CARD 9	This is what you hope or fear, perhaps what you both want *and* fear.
CARD 10	This is what will come and describes the likely future outcome.

Home Life and You: The Feng Shui Spread

This pattern represents the eight-sided octagon called a bagua, used by feng shui practitioners to examine the connections between a person's home and his or her life. The cards show the energies and influences operating in each area of the person's life:

CARD 1	Fame, future, career
CARD 2	Relationships, marriage, partnerships
CARD 3	Creativity, children
CARD 4	Helpful people, friends, agents/associates/colleagues, travel
CARD 5	Self, identity, image
CARD 6	Wisdom, knowledge, spirituality
CARD 7	Family, community, neighbors
CARD 8	Wealth
CARD 9	Health

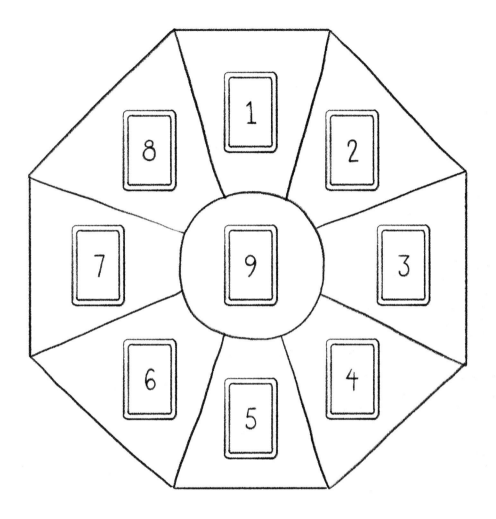

The Feng Shui Spread

Horoscope Spread: Astrology Lends a Hand

In this spread, twelve cards are laid out in a circle. Each card corresponds to one of the twelve houses of the astrological chart. A thirteenth card, a Significator, can be placed in the center if you want.

Each house refers to a specific area of life; thus, the cards are read in reference to the house in which they fall. For instance, an Ace in the second house indicates a new moneymaking opportunity or project; an Ace in the seventh describes the beginning of a relationship. This spread is not generally used to answer specific questions—it provides an overview of the person's life at the time of the reading. The person's sun sign or birth chart are not factors in a reading that uses this spread.

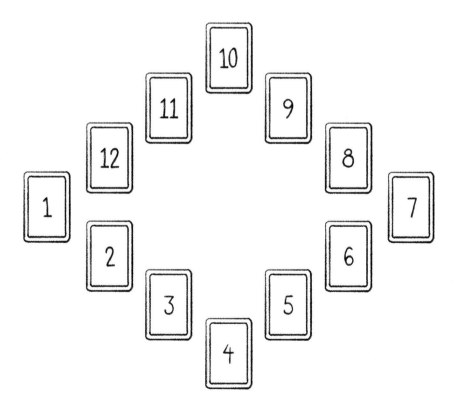

The First House: The Self

The first house begins at the nine o'clock position, and the cards are dealt counterclockwise. The first house refers to the physical body and appearance, as well as your vitality, identity, sense of self, and the immediate impression you make on others.

The Second House: Personal Resources

The second house shows what you consider valuable. This includes money, personal possessions, resources, earning ability, and your identification with what you own.

The Third House: The Near Environment

The third house covers three areas of life that at first may not seem related, but taken together represent normal daily life, or what astrologers call the near environment—communications related to the routine of everyday life; involvement with friends, neighbors, siblings, and the community at large; and short-distance travel in your near environment.

The Fourth House: Roots

The fourth house represents the foundation of your life—home, family, parents (especially the mother), tradition, heritage, the past, your homeland—in short, your roots.

The Fifth House: Self-Expression

The fifth house shows your creative and self-expressive side, which may play out as artistic endeavors, romantic relationships, hobbies, or children.

The Sixth House: Health and Service

The sixth house relates to health, health-oriented routines including nutrition and exercise, and the link between work and health. It also describes your daily work or chores, duties, job-oriented relationships, service to others, and capacity for self-sacrifice.

The Seventh House: One-on-One Relationships

Traditionally the house of marriage and partnerships, the seventh represents all one-on-one relationships—business and personal, including relationships with known enemies.

The Eighth House: Transformation

The eighth is the house of the past, transformative change, death, inheritance, and other people's resources. In this case, death usually refers to the end of something old so that something new can emerge, not necessarily the death of a person. The eighth house also shows how another's resources affect you.

The Ninth House: Higher Knowledge

The ninth house represents the higher mind, philosophy, religion/spirituality, the law, and advanced education, as well as long-distance travel, especially to foreign lands. This house shows your search for meaning and how you go about expanding your horizons and knowledge of the world.

The Tenth House: Life Task

The tenth house represents social or professional status, career, public image, and parents (the father especially). Authority, responsibilities, honor, and reputation are tenth-house matters too.

The Eleventh House: Friendships

The eleventh house refers to your friends and groups with which you are affiliated. Goals, hopes, and wishes are shown by this house too.

The Twelfth House: The Hidden Realm

The twelfth house represents that which is hidden, or not yet revealed, including your dreams and fantasies. It also reveals your as-yet-unused talents as well as fears, weaknesses, secrets, and unknown enemies. Because matters associated with this sector are often unknown to you, the house is sometimes connected with self-undoing.

Chapter
7

PRACTICAL TAROT: USING TAROT IN YOUR EVERYDAY LIFE

TAROT ETHICS: READING FOR OTHER PEOPLE

What will you do when you are at a party and someone asks if you can give her a tarot reading to figure out if she will get a cash windfall from a lawsuit? Or someone wants you to do a reading to assess whether he will get brain cancer like his father did. It is helpful to have at least some inkling of how you would react in this type of scenario.

A hot topic in the tarot community always centers around tarot ethics—when is it okay to do a tarot reading and when is it best to pass. You need to come up with your own list of what type of readings you are comfortable doing and in what circumstances you would rather leave the cards alone. It is important to think about these situations before you encounter them so you do not have to make a rash decision in the moment.

There are no right or wrong answers as to what to do in these different situations—well, unless your local laws or ordinances have clearly outlined them for you. You can always change your mind later on if you have an encounter that sways you one way or the other.

Be Careful with Medical and Legal Advice

Many tarot readers refuse to answer questions from other people that could be construed as medical or legal advice. A person may come to you wondering why he has pain in his abdomen or if she sued her neighbor, how likely would she be to win. Decide for yourself if you are comfortable answering these questions and what the laws in your area would allow. (It is acceptable to use the cards to guide your own medical issues.)

A common issue for tarot readers who read during parties or events is to run into individuals who are drunk and would like to receive a tarot reading. Some clients may even come to you after having a few drinks to settle their nerves before a reading. Would you rather pass on reading for someone who has had a few drinks, or are you okay reading for individuals who might not be at their sharpest?

Young Clients

It is also important to decide how you would like to handle doing tarot readings for individuals under eighteen. Some local laws may prohibit this type of reading, so be sure to do your research. If you are interested in doing readings for minors, think about if you want to get their parents' approval first or if you want one of their parents to sit in on the reading.

Friends and Family

Even if you are not planning on reading tarot professionally, when people learn that you are interested in the field you will likely have family and friends asking you to do readings for them. Before saying yes, think about it carefully. Sometimes information will come up in a reading that is sensitive or private. Your friend may think the reading is just fun and not realize that you are potentially peeking into her soul. Doing readings for family and friends can potentially change your relationships with them. Decide if you are okay with this.

USING TAROT FOR YOUR OWN SPIRITUAL GUIDANCE

Whether you do readings on others or not, you probably want to use tarot as a tool for personal growth. Some decks, such as the Jungian Tarot and the Starchild Tarot, are designed specifically to augment spiritual and psychological development. Of course, any deck—and any reading—can reveal important personal issues you need to address, and often does. Many spreads are designed to take into account the emotional, spiritual, and mental dynamics that are affecting the subject of the reading, but you can intentionally choose to work with tarot to understand and heal particular problems in your life.

◆ **TAROT TIP**

Taking a tarot deck with you to your therapist appointment may also be help-ful to get ideas of what areas would be beneficial to explore and where to look deeper into your life. These two worlds aren't always separate—several well-known individuals in the tarot community are also practicing psycholo-gists. It is a field that seems to attract interest in the occult, especially tarot.

When using tarot to examine your spiritual journey, it is helpful to journal each encounter. After completing a reading for yourself, note how you feel and what emotions or experiences come up after the reading.

MEDITATING WITH TAROT CARDS

Meditating with tarot cards is a simple and relaxing way to connect with your intuition. The simplest way to do this is to select a single card that represents an issue you are dealing with and remove it from the deck.

If you feel vulnerable or uncertain in a romantic relationship, for instance, you might choose the Page of Cups to contemplate. If you are embroiled in ego battles with coworkers, pick the Five of Wands. Or choose a card that symbolizes a characteristic you wish to develop in yourself. Strength, for example, can help you build inner power, patience, and perseverance. The Queen of Cups can encourage receptivity, acceptance, and flexibility in relationships.

Relax, take a deep breath, clear your mind, and center yourself, then gaze at the image on the card, without trying to analyze it too closely. Allow the symbols pictured there to speak directly to your subconscious. They will trigger an inner awareness and gently work on the conditions that are influencing the situation. As the card's meaning imprints itself on your mind, you will notice the traits you desire becoming more available to you, and/or you'll experience an increased ability to handle the situation that is challenging you.

 TAROT TIP

Continue meditating on a chosen card day after day, until you have resolved the concern or developed the qualities you want. You could also display the card in a place where you will see it often throughout the day. Each time you look at it, you'll be reminded of your intention.

IS YOUR INNER KNOWING TRYING TO TELL YOU SOMETHING?

Tarot cards can also help you to diagnose difficulties—physical as well as psychological. Let's say, for example, that you are experiencing lower back pain. You could ask the tarot, "What factors are involved in this condition?" Then randomly draw one or more cards from the deck. In this instance, you might pick the Three of Swords, which suggests that your back pain is linked with the emotional pain of a recent breakup. If you drew the Ten of Wands, you might determine that carrying a heavy load—either physically or personally—caused the problem.

Allow your intuition to guide you. Don't necessarily stick to standard interpretations; whatever pops into your mind could be meaningful. Maybe you picked The Star in response to a query about a sore throat that's been bothering you. This card usually represents hope—it probably indicates that your sore throat isn't serious and you will soon be fine. But if The Star card in your deck depicts a woman kneeling in water, it could be telling you that your malady is connected with getting wet and chilled.

You can also use the cards as aids to healing. The Nine of Wands, for example, is considered a card of recovery. Gaze at it when you are ill and breathe in its vibrations to facilitate well-being. Or lay it on an injury to send positive energy to the wound. Some people like to position seven beneficial cards on their bodies at the seven chakra points. Although this method is certainly not a substitute for qualified medical care, the cards can often shed light on situations and may offer guidance for healing problems.

USE YOUR CREATIVITY TO CREATE YOUR OWN DECK

Creating your own deck is the ultimate tarot experience. Whether or not you believe you have artistic ability, you can embark on this journey of self-expression and discovery. Choose whatever medium appeals to you—watercolors, acrylic, oils, pen and ink, colored pencils, pastels, woodcut, collage, fabric, crayons, digital art, or another medium. Give yourself permission to experiment. What matters is that the images reflect your own interpretations of the cards.

Creating your personal tarot deck requires you to design seventy-eight individual pictures, unless you opt to do only the twenty-two Major Arcana cards. It's a long project, but you can do it in small spurts of time and enjoy your progress.

> ### ◆ TAROT TIP
>
> When designing your own personal tarot deck, you may want to start with cards that depict conditions you wish to attract into your life. For example, you could focus on creating positive cards.

One way to approach the design process is to work on cards that represent issues that are currently in the forefront of your life. For instance, if you are resting and recuperating after an illness or injury, you might relate to the Four of Swords and decide to depict it first. As you create the card, you'll come to a deeper understanding of the situation you are experiencing, and your understanding will naturally be transferred to the card's imagery.

However you decide to go about creating your own tarot deck, you will find the experience illuminating. Invite your muse to participate and guide you. Don't judge or censor yourself. Be daring—there are no rules here. Allow for serendipity to enter into the process and above all enjoy yourself!

CREATING YOUR OWN TAROT SPREADS

Once you are comfortable using traditional tarot spreads to answer questions, you can start to create your own spreads. Spreads can be specific to a situation, or broad to fit multiple circumstances. It is a relatively simple process, made even easier after you are familiar with the types of questions that tarot answers best—questions that are open-ended and not the simple "yes or no" variety.

To create your own personal tarot spread, come up with a list of questions that you would like answered. Some topics you might like to explore are the general energy of the subject, advice on how to handle a situation, the outcome expected, and so forth. Then decide on a configuration that will best help you see a broader overview of how the questions relate.

Generally, past events go to the left and future events go to the right, so you can read the answer like a story. If you want to know what you need to do to help a situation grow, place the card with the action you need to take underneath a Significator card. Then place a card over the Significator card to reveal how a situation will "grow" after you have "planted the seeds."

Many readers also like to come up with signature go-to spreads to use when asking a generic question. Play around with the types of questions you like the best and come up with a configuration of the cards that is personal to you. If you like stars, maybe you can fashion a spread that looks like a star. Perhaps you would like an arrow-shaped reading to tell how to best move forward in your life.

The most important thing to keep in mind when creating a spread is to have fun! Don't get too overwhelmed with the process. Let your intuition guide you.

TRUST YOURSELF

Thank you for taking this journey through *The Only Tarot Book You'll Ever Need*. Tarot is a powerful tool that you can use to unlock the hidden secrets of your unconscious and to tap into that divine spark inside yourself. Tarot can be used in so many different ways—from telling someone's fortune to understanding deep psychological aspects of your personality.

Remember, using tarot should be a fun experience. When you are truly tapping into your essence, it is an act of self-love and personal development. Trust yourself and let tarot guide you on your journey to spiritual fulfillment. ◆

INDEX